Eggbert, the Ball, Bounces by Himself

Caught'ya! Grammar with a Giggle for First Grade

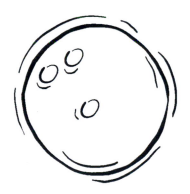

Jane Bell Kiester

Eggbert, the Ball, Bounces by Himself
Caught'ya! Grammar with a Giggle for First Grade

By Jane Bell Kiester

Cover design: David J. Dishman
Book design: Billie J. Hermansen
Editor: Emily Gorovsky

Library of Congress Cataloging-in-Publication Data

Kiester, Jane Bell, 1945-
   Eggbert, the ball, bounces by himself : Caught'ya! grammar with a giggle
for first grade / Jane Bell Kiester.
       p. cm.
   Includes bibliographical references.
   ISBN: 978-0-929895-02-4 (pbk.)
   1. English language—Grammar—Study and teaching (Primary) 2. Humor in
education. 3. First grade (Education) I. Title.
   LB1528.K52 2006
   372.61—dc22
                         2006012649

Also by Jane Bell Kiester
   Blowing Away the State Writing Assessment Test: Four Steps to Better Writing Scores for Students of All Levels
   Caught'ya! Grammar with a Giggle
   Caught'ya Again! More Grammar with a Giggle
   The Chortling Bard: Caught'ya! Grammar with a Giggle for High School
   Giggles in the Middle: Caught'ya! Grammar with a Giggle for Middle School
   Juan and Marie Join the Class: Caught'ya! Grammar with a Giggle for Third Grade
   Putrescent Petra Finds Friends: Caught'ya! Grammar with a Giggle for Second Grade

Maupin House publishes professional resources for K-12 educators. Contact us for tailored, in-school training or to schedule an author for a workshop or conference. Visit www.maupinhouse.com for free lesson plan downloads.

Maupin House Publishing, Inc. by Capstone Professional
1710 Roe Crest Drive
North Mankato, MN 56003
www.maupinhouse.com
888-262-6135
info@maupinhouse.com

DEDICATION

For Isabelle, my adored granddaughter. You are my favorite first-grader in the whole world. You light up my life with your laugh. Grandma loves you forever and always.

and

For all you brave and wonderful souls who love to teach first grade.
You are the foundation onto which the rest of us build.

ACKNOWLEDGMENTS

First, I wish to thank my constant, loving editors—my mother, Perra Bell, and my husband, Chuck Kiester. Without your editing and "tersing," not to mention encouragement, I would not dare write. I love you.

Second, I wish to thank the six teachers at Tommy Barfield Elementary School who teach in two multi-age, primary-program teams. They shared their expertise, ideas, and enthusiasm. Debbie Cooper, Jody McCarty, and Esther Scuderi taught one combined kindergarten/first-grade/second-grade class. Margo Barath, Diane Stone, and Barbara Stukey taught the second multi-age group. Thank you, ladies; you're super! Congratulations on the continued, high Florida Writes! scores at your school.

I especially with to thank Debbie Cooper who spoke to me at length about the magic she and her colleagues weave to teach students how to write correctly and confidently. Debbie also gave me some wonderful examples of her students' work and tested parts of this book with her class.

A special thank you goes again to Diane Stone for her help with the example of a student in her multi-age classroom. I also want to thank Robert Voorhees for donating his work to this book. Robert, you were a real help! Your example is perfect.

Thank you also to my beloved granddaughter, Isabelle, who patiently listened to and approved Eggbert's story at age five and then read it all by herself when she reached first grade. Grandma thinks that you are amazing and wonderful! Thank you for your help and your hugs.

And finally, I wish to thank my superb editor, Emily Gorovsky. I so appreciate your organizational expertise. Isn't it nice we're on the same page?

TABLE OF CONTENTS

IN THE BOOK

ON THE CD

An Introduction by Jane Bell Kiester

Eight Steps to Implement Caught'yas in Your
Classroom Explained

"Eggbert, the Ball, Bounces by Himself," the entire,
uninterrupted Caught'ya story

Student Caught'yas (formatted one per page)

Student Assessment Chart

Two First-Grade Caught'ya Examples

Seven Writing Suggestions and Activities

*Grammar, Usage, and Mechanics Guide
(Everything You Never Wanted to Know about
Grammar, Usage, and Mechanics,
but I'm Going to Tell You Anyway)*

WHAT YOU WILL FIND IN THIS BOOK

The Caught'ya method teaches grammar, mechanics, usage, and vocabulary, all within the context of a story. Each Caught'ya, or story segment is one to four sentences long. Each segment has an error-laden "S" (for student) sentence with its corresponding, corrected "C" sentence that will serve as your teacher key. A list of skills is included above each Caught'ya for you to note what is being covered and what may need extra review. All vocabulary not on the Dolch Word List for first grade is listed before the Caught'yas so that you will know what words you may want to emphasize as they come up in your students' reading.

This **book** and the accompanying **CD** contain everything you need to use the Caught'ya method successfully with your first-grade students. In the book, you will find the following sections.

Caught'yas in a Nutshell briefly explains the Caught'ya method and lists eight easy steps for implementing the method in your class.

"Eggbert, the Ball, Bounces by Himself," the entire, uninterrupted Caught'ya story, is printed so that you can familiarize yourself with the plot before you start the Caught'yas. Numbers displayed in the margin of the story correspond with the number of the Caught'ya for easy reference.

120 Student Caught'yas with Teacher's Key includes the student ("S") sentences and corrected ("C") sentences as well as a list of skills and bolded vocabulary for each Caught'ya.

On the **CD**, you'll find files that save you time, allow you to customize the Caught'yas to your needs, provide additional explanation, and present effective teaching ideas to supplement the daily Caught'yas.

An Introduction by Jane Bell Kiester shares the history of Caught'yas, why they're so successful, and how the method specifically works with first-graders.

Eight Steps to Implement Caught'yas in Your Classroom Explained will regale you with all the details and tricks necessary for implementing the Caught'ya method in your classroom.

"Eggbert, the Ball, Bounces by Himself," the entire, uninterrupted Caught'ya story, is included so that you can print a copy to have in your classroom if you wish.

Student Caught'yas are provided so that you do not have to copy or type the Caught'yas and so that you easily can modify the sentences to fit your students' needs. There is one Caught'ya per page so that you can make booklets for your students' use.

The **Student Assessment Chart** lets you track students' writing progress and note areas that need improvement.

Two First-Grade Caught'ya Examples show you what student Caught'yas from Eggbert's story and a thematic unit look like.

Seven Writing Suggestions and Activities help your students master the different types of prose in fun, effective, classroom-proven ways.

The ***Grammar, Usage, and Mechanics Guide*** (*Everything You Never Wanted to Know about Grammar, Usage, and Mechanics, but I'm Going to Tell You Anyway*) is a useful addendum I referred to almost daily when I taught Caught'yas (and I wrote it). The ***GUM Guide*** and the Caught'yas cover every skill listed in *Warriner's English Grammar and Composition: Complete Course*—the big white book that bored so many of us when we were in school. While in the first grade, you will not be teaching most of the skills listed and illustrated in this guide, you might find it useful for reference and teaching ideas. You can use it on the **CD** or print out a copy to put in your book.

Besides providing a quick reference for you, the ***GUM Guide*** contains simple examples you can use in your instruction and mnemonic devices to help your students learn some of the more difficult concepts.

Now I invite you to relax and read the rest of this book. I wish you and your students many giggles, a plethora of great vocabulary words, and much fluent writing.

CAUGHT'YAS IN A NUTSHELL

A QUICK OVERVIEW OF THE CAUGHT'YA METHOD FOR FIRST GRADE

The Caught'ya method teaches language skills in context in an integrated approach, making certain to cover all (and more) of your state's standards for the first-grade level. Essentially, a Caught'ya is one to four sentences of an ongoing, funny story taught every day from a blackboard or overhead and corrected by students in their editing journals (simply a booklet that contains the Caught'yas you run off from the CD).

In this book, there is a story that is specifically designed for first grade. There are the student sentences, the teacher's key, and a list of the skills being taught in the Caught'ya. Each Caught'ya contains cloze blanks (where strategic letters in words have been omitted) and simple errors (like no period at the end of the sentence or a missing capital letter at the beginning). This is designed to move stage three writers (letter copiers) to subsequent writing stages and make it possible for *all* students to experience success. (See the student examples at the end of this section and full-size on the CD.) Each Caught'ya also includes several challenging words (those not on the Dolch Sight Word List for first grade) which should be new to most students. A few Caught'yas also contain simple literary devices such as similes.

Before your students begin working on a Caught'ya, you need to do the following:

➔ Review what happened in the story so far (you can read the uninterrupted Caught'ya story up to the point of the last Caught'ya);

➔ Introduce and elicit the meanings of the vocabulary word(s);

➔ Read the Caught'ya dramatically;

➔ Carefully repeat any word in which there are cloze blanks;

➔ Point out the spaces between words;

➔ Go over the need for a capital letter at the beginning of a sentence and a period at the end (use kinesthetic techniques explained in **Step 4** of **Eight Steps to Implement Caught'yas in Your Classroom Explained** on the CD); and

➔ Initiate a discussion of whether to begin a new paragraph in the story.

You can modify the skills to fit the needs of your students by changing the Caught'yas on the CD, such as adding a simile, leaving out or adding punctuation, or inserting more cloze blanks.

Each student has a copy of the Caught'ya to correct (see the CD) in their editing journals with room underneath to draw a picture that illustrates the meaning of the sentence(s). As students complete the Caught'ya, you walk around the room and give immediate, tinged-with-humor feedback (hugs included) to each student, hint at missing punctuation by using kinesthetic techniques, provide quick mini-lessons, help those who are not developmentally past stage four writing (the labelers), and urge or challenge students to find the errors and letters on their own.

Then, in their response journals, students write about any topic they wish using as many words and letters as they can. Or, they write about a topic you come up with that is related to something in the Caught'ya. Please note that, in the **Eight Steps to Implement Caught'yas in Your Classroom Explained** on the CD, editing and response journals will be explained in much more detail, including several ways to make the journals and establish their use in your classroom.

When nearly all of the students have completed the Caught'ya, drawn the picture that demonstrates comprehension, "written" in their response journals, and received a comment from you, you return to the board or overhead. Together, you and students again discuss the meanings of the vocabulary words, acting them out if possible.

Then, with you presiding, the entire class reads the Caught'ya again several times and reviews the missing letters (cloze blanks), missing punctuation, and capitalization errors. Discuss as much as possible at this point, including the *reasons* and *rules* for each correction.

Caught'yas will be successful in your classroom if you are at all enthusiastic about them and about the subsequent improvement in your students' writing. Please keep in mind that the most important elements are humor, enthusiasm, playing with the vocabulary, and student success.

EVALUATING THE CAUGHT'YAS

Evaluating the Caught'yas is as important as doing them. It is based on whether students catch the errors and mark them on their papers when the class reviews the sentences together, *not* on the number of errors made when students attempted to correct the Caught'ya on their own. In this way, no matter how weak their English skills are, students can experience success with this method. Your weakest students can excel if they listen and carefully correct their work. This is a wonderful inducement to pay attention.

You will want to collect the editing and response journals on a weekly basis, check them for errors, monitor students' writing fluency, and make positive comments in each child's journals. I suggest you keep a chart on each child's progress (see the sample **Student Assessment Chart** on the CD) that tracks the skills mastered, the number of more sophisticated vocabulary words used, and the increase in the number of sentences written (and subsequent decrease in the use of pictures and letters). As you fill in the chart week after week, you will be delighted at the improvement in your students' writing ability.

EIGHT STEPS TO IMPLEMENT CAUGHT'YAS IN YOUR CLASSROOM

(For more detailed instructions, see **Eight Steps to Implement Caught'yas in Your Classroom Explained** on the CD.)

1. Read the complete Caught'ya story, "Eggbert, the Ball, Bounces by Himself"; buy several balls that can be classroom Eggberts; and plan to do a Caught'ya every day from Eggbert's story, your own sentences, or a thematic unit of your choice.

2. Decide on skills and vocabulary words you want to include, change the student sentences on the CD accordingly, and insert your students' names in the blanks provided. Then, run off a copy of the Caught'yas, ten at a time, turning them into small booklets of ten Caught'yas each for every student.

3. Teach your students about editing and response journals, and make or buy one of each for every student. Read the introduction to Eggbert's story to your class.

4. The day before doing a Caught'ya, introduce that Caught'ya's vocabulary. The next day, write the Caught'ya on the board or overhead. Read the Caught'ya dramatically, go over the vocabulary words again, identify the missing letters in the cloze blanks, and review capitalization and end punctuation using kinesthetic techniques.

5. For each Caught'ya in their editing journals, students fill in the cloze blanks, put in any missing punctuation or capital letters, draw a picture to illustrate the content, and, with as many letters and words as they can, "write" something related to the Caught'ya in their response journals.

6. Walk around the room, commenting on each student's effort, giving hugs, and helping with response journals.

7. Check the Caught'ya orally with the class at the board or overheard, eliciting answers from students and reviewing vocabulary. Go over vocabulary for the next day's Caught'ya.

8. Collect the editing journals, and make positive comments. Note common errors your students make for later instruction. Collect response journals, and write encouraging comments by at least one entry. Track each student's writing progress in their response journals using the Student Assessment Chart on the CD.

Your name Robert

Super work, Robert! You even put the ? in "teacher's."

Day and date Tuesday, March 8, 2005

83. **children   high**

⌈eggbert rolled out from under the big desk of the teacher. he bounced up and down, up and d_o_ _w_ _n_ so he could see all the **children**. he b_o_ _u_ _n_ _c_ _e_ _d_ so **high**, he went right onto the teacher'_s_ desk.

Example #1: First-Grade Caught'ya ("Eggbert, the Ball, Bounces by Himself")

19. Mangroves provide a habitat and food for animals above and below the water.

Actual work of first grade student in Editing Journal

Example #2: First-Grade Caught'ya (Thematic Unit)

"EGGBERT, THE BALL, BOUNCES BY HIMSELF," THE ENTIRE, UNINTERRUPTED CAUGHT'YA STORY

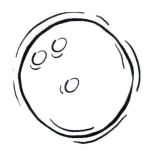

NOTE: The numbers in the margin correspond with the Caught'yas.

It was dark in the toy store. It was quiet. Toys sat on long gray **shelves**. On the wall, a clock tick-tocked. The clock tick-tocked so softly you could **barely** hear it. The **toy store** was closed and locked up for the night.

Suddenly, at the end of one of the rows of shelves, near the far wall of the store, a light **flickered** on and off, on and off like Tinkerbell. There was a sound like a small bell. Something rolled on a shelf and fell to the floor with a small thump.

Whatever it was sat there a minute. Then it **bounced**, slowly at first, then faster and faster and higher and higher. It **arrived** at the front of the store. It bounced one more time up into the big front window of the store. There it stopped. It made a noise from the **valve** in its side. (***Show a valve and explain its use.***) The noise sounded like a **sigh**.

What had bounced all on its own without boy or girl hands to move it? What had sighed? What was in the big window of the toy store? A ball!

This ball was round like all other balls. It did not look much different from all other balls. This ball was... (***Insert your own description of the ball you have in your classroom.***)

But, this was no ordinary ball. This ball was **special**. This ball had a name—**Eggbert**. This ball could bounce all by itself! This ball could think. This ball even could **understand** people talking! Eggbert was special.

Now, Eggbert did not know how or why he was different from all the other balls. He just was. One minute he had been on the shelf with all the other balls. He did not think. He could not more. Then a light had flickered on and off like Tinkerbell. All of a sudden Eggbert could think. He could move by himself.

Now, Eggbert had rolled and bounced himself to the big front window of the store. He wanted to see what was outside the store. You see, none of the toys knew what was outside the store.

They saw the inside of a **factory**. Then they saw the inside of a big brown box. Then they saw the inside of the toy store. No toy in the store had ever been outside in the big world.

This was why the minute Eggbert knew he could bounce all by himself, he bounced his way to the front **window**. He had always been **jealous** of the lucky toys who sat in the window. They could see outside.

Eggbert sat the rest of the night in the toy store window. He was **waiting**. He did not know what he was waiting for. But, Eggbert waited anyway...

Eggbert **sat** and **sat**. It was dark **inside**. It was black **outside**. The black **outside** went away. The sun came up. It looked like a big ball, a big yellow ball **high** in the sky. The sun was **bright** and pretty. The sun was big and yellow. Eggbert looked around. Eggbert looked **outside** the **window**. He looked and looked. Eggbert saw **boys** and **girls** run by. Big, tall **people** went by. Short, fat **people** went by. _____ and _____ and _____ ran by. No one saw Eggbert. No one **stopped** to look in the **window**. Eggbert looked and looked. He saw **boys** and **girls**. He saw dogs and cats. A **boy** ran by. A **girl** ran by. A big dog ran by. A black and white cat with long white **whiskers** looked at Eggbert. It said, "**Meow**." The cat was **outside**. Eggbert was not **outside**. He was **inside**.

Eggbert **wanted** to **roll** and **bounce** with the **boys** and **girls**. He **wanted** to go with them. He **wanted** to **feel** the sun.

"I want to be with them," Eggbert said. "I want to **roll** and **bounce** with them. I want to see the **outside**."

Eggbert **sighed**. He **sighed** and **sighed**. Then a tall man came to the **door** of the **store**. The tall man **opened** the **door**. He came in the **toy store**. He did not see Eggbert in the big **window**. The man went to the **back** of the **store**. Eggbert saw him look around. Eggbert **bounced** up and down, up and down, up and down three (3) **times**. The man did not see Eggbert bounce by **himself**. Eggbert **sighed** and **sighed**. He **wanted** the man to see him. The man did not see him. The man did not see Eggbert. The man did not **hear** Eggbert. The man worked in the **toy store**. He liked to work in the **toy store**.
It was fun.

Eggbert **sat** in the **window** all day. Then it got **dark outside**. Eggbert **sat** in the **window** all **night**. No one saw Eggbert. No one **heard** Eggbert. Only a black and white cat looked at Eggbert. Can you **hear** a ball **sigh**?

Eggbert was very sad. Eggbert was very **lonely**. One **night** he **bounced** out of the **window** into the **store**.

"I will **bounce** and **roll**," Eggbert said one **night**. "The man will see me. **Boys** and **girls** will see me."

One day the man **found** Eggbert on the **floor**. He put Eggbert **back** in the **window**. He did not **talk** to Eggbert. One day the man **found** Eggbert **high** up on a **shelf**. He put Eggbert **back** in the **window**.

Every day the man **found** Eggbert out of the **window**. What a **strange** ball! Where would the ball be **every** day when the man came to work? Every day the man put Eggbert **back** in the window. Every **night** Eggbert **bounced** out of the **window**.

"This ball **is special**," the man said.

Eggbert **bounced** up and down, up and down, up and down three (3) **times** to say "Yes." Did the **nice** man see Eggbert **bounce** by **himself**? No. Eggbert was sad.

One day a **nice lady** came in the **store**. She looked **a lot** like your **teacher**. Who was she? What did she want? This **lady** looked **nice**. She looked **kind**. Eggbert was **excited**. The **lady** looked around the **toy store**. She looked in the **back** of the **store**. She looked in the **front** of the **store**.

Eggbert **sighed** and **sighed**. He **bounced** up and down. "Please see me. Please see me," he wanted to say. "Please take me with you. Please take me with you."

The **lady** saw Eggbert. She saw him bounce up and down. She **heard** him **sigh through** his **valve**.

The **lady** said to the man in the store, "I want to **buy** this ball. This ball is **special**. To Eggbert she said, "How my **children** at (**put your school name here**) would like to have you in their **classroom**!"

Eggbert **rolled** up and down. He **rolled** to the **left** and then to the **right**. He was happy. He was full of **joy**. Why was Eggbert happy? **Someone noticed** him. Someone **talked** to him. Eggbert wished he **could talk back**.

Eggbert **sighed**. He let **air** come **through** his **valve** with a **hiss** like a **snake**. The **lady** heard him, and she was very **excited**.

"Oh, you **talk**," she **cried** out with joy. "You **hiss** like a **snake**, and you bounce and **roll** all by yourself. What **else** can you do?" she asked Eggbert.

Eggbert bounced five **times**. He bounced right up to the kind **lady**, **rolled** onto her **feet**, and let out a **hiss**. Eggbert wanted the **lady** to take him **home** with her. Eggbert bounced again, right on the **lady's feet**. Then he bounced two times, even **higher**. On the next bounce, Eggbert jumped into the nice **lady's arms**.

"Oh," said the **lady** to Eggbert. "I want to buy you. How much do you **cost**?"

Eggbert **hissed**. He **rolled** around in the **lady's arms** so she could see his **tag**.

"Your name is Eggbert," said the **lady**. "It says so right on your **tag**. "Hello, Eggbert. My name is (**put your name here**). You are **going** to laugh, **hiss**, and play with my **children**."

(**Put your name here**) **paid** for Eggbert and **took** him outside in her **arms**. She did not put Eggbert in a **bag**. She **knew** he wanted to see outside the **store**. (**Put your name here**) and Eggbert went out of the toy store, and they got into a little yellow **car** with green **doors**. (**Put your name here**) put Eggbert in the **back** so that he could see out the big **back window**.

"Just don't roll off of the **shelf**," said the lady to Eggbert. "If you roll off the **shelf**, you won't be able to see out the **window**," she **explained**.

Eggbert bounced three little bounces to say, "Yes." He bounced very **carefully**. He did not want to fall off this **shelf**. *This* shelf had a **window** to the outside.

Eggbert looked and looked. He saw **other cars** ride down the **road**. Some went very fast. Some went very **slowly**. Eggbert liked the slow cars best. He could see **people** and dogs inside them. He did not see **other** balls. A big brown dog in a big blue car put its head out the **window**. It **barked** at Eggbert as he **rode** by.

"**Bark. Bark**," the dog said.

Eggbert wanted to **bark back** at the dog. He bounced, and he **hissed**, but he could not **bark**.

Oh, Eggbert," said (*put your name here*), "You are a ball. You are not a dog. Balls do not **bark**.

Eggbert saw a little girl in a big red **car**. Her **name** was _____. The girl **waved** and laughed to see the ball in the **back window** of a little yellow and green **car**. Eggbert wanted to **wave** and laugh, too.

He bounced up and down, up and down, ten **times**. This is how a ball **waves** to you. Eggbert **tried** to laugh, but it **sounded** like a **hiss**.

"Oh, Eggbert," said (*put your name here*). "You will run out of **air** if you **hiss** and **hiss**. Eggbert *was* looking a little **flat**.

"Here we are," said (*put your name here*).

Eggbert looked out the back **window**. He saw a big red **building**. It was a **school**.

"This is our **school**," said (*put your name here*) to Eggbert. "You will **live** here in my **classroom**. I have a **shelf** just for you."

The lady stopped the little yellow car with the green **doors**. She stopped right in **front** of the red **school**. Eggbert was very **excited**.

Eggbert was so **excited**. He bounced, and he **hissed**. He **hissed** so much, he was almost **flat** when (*put your name here*) **picked** him up from the **back** of the car.

"You made yourself **flat**," said (*put your name here*). "You **hissed** too much. I can **fix** that. I will **blow air** into your **valve**."

Eggbert **could** not hiss. He was too **flat**. **Poor** Eggbert **could** not bounce. He was too **flat**. Do you go **flat** when you try to talk?

(*Put your name here*) walked into the red **school**. She took Eggbert down a long **hall**. She opened a brown **door**. Eggbert saw **a lot** of little **desks**.

"This is our **classroom**," she said. "**Boys** and **girls** come here **every** day. They will play with you. They will **love** you."

Then she walked up to a big **desk**. Many **papers covered** the **desk**. The **desk** was a **mess**. Is your **teacher's desk** a **mess**? Is your **desk** a **mess**?

(*Put your name here*) put Eggbert on her **messy desk**. "Soon," she said, "many **children** will come into this **classroom**."

Eggbert looked around the **classroom**. He saw many funny **things**. He **heard** funny **noises**.

What did Eggbert see? Draw a **picture** (with some words) of your **classroom** to show what Eggbert saw. How many windows did Eggbert see?

Eggbert saw **a lot** of **desks**. How many **desks** did Eggbert see?

"I want to bounce on every **desk**," Eggbert said to himself.

He **tried** to bounce, but he could not. Eggbert was too **flat**.

The nice **lady** saw Eggbert try to bounce. "Oh," she said, "I **need** to put **air** into you."

The **lady** put Eggbert's **valve** up to her lips. She **blew**, and she **blew**.

"This will **fix** you," she said to Eggbert as she **blew air** into his **valve**.

Eggbert **rolled** in her hands. It **tickled** when (*put your name here*) **blew air** into his **valve**.

 He grew and grew as she **blew**.

The nice lady picked up some **papers** from her desk. One **paper** was right under Eggbert.

"I'm **sorry**," she said to Eggbert. "Did that **tickle** you?"

Eggbert bounced up and down three **times** to say, "Yes."

The nice lady laughed. Eggbert laughed, too, with a little hiss. He wanted to say, "Thank you," but he could not **talk**. He could only hiss like a **snake**.

Then the kind lady **left** the **classroom**. As she went out the door, she **waved** to Eggbert.

"Good-bye," she said. "Don't fall off the **desk**." Then she said, "I will be back **tomorrow** when the sun comes up. Be a good ball."

When the **door closed**, it was **quiet** in the **classroom**. Eggbert was all by himself. He was **lonely**. Then Eggbert saw a **door inside** the **classroom**. Where did it go? What was **behind** the **door**? Who was **behind** the **door**?

"Today was a big day for a ball who has never been outside. I will sleep here on the big **desk**," **thought** Eggbert. "Then I will look around **tomorrow**. I can bounce and hiss again now that I am round and full of air again."

Eggbert went to sleep right there on the **teacher's desk**.

The **next morning** a **loud bell woke** up Eggbert. It was very **loud**. Eggbert was so surprised, he **fell** off the **desk**.

When the **bell rang** again, Eggbert **rolled** under the **teacher's desk**. He was **still** there when (***put your name here***) came into the **classroom**.

"Where are you, Eggbert?" She called when she did not see the ball. "I want to wash you. I must get you **ready** for my **students**."

(***Put your name here***) looked **everywhere** for Eggbert. She looked under all the little **desks**. She looked on all the **shelves**. She looked in the **bathroom**, too. She did not see Eggbert. "Where is that ball?" she said.

Just then _____, _____, and _____ came into the **classroom**.

"What are you looking for?" _____ asked her **teacher**.

"I am looking for Eggbert," said the **teacher**.

"Who is Eggbert?" asked _____.

"Eggbert is a **surprise**," said _____.

"Do you want me to help you look?" asked _____.

"Yes," said the **teacher**.

"Can I help, too?" asked _____ and _____ as they walked in the door.

"Yes, you can help, too," said the **teacher**.

The six looked **everywhere**. Just then _____ and _____ came in the classroom door.

"What is that **funny-looking** round **thing** under your desk?" _____ asked his **teacher**.

"That must be Eggbert," said the **teacher**. "Come out, Eggbert."

Eggbert rolled out from under her desk.

"Oh, what a pretty ball!" said _____ and _____ together.

The **bell rang** again, and many **children** ran into the classroom. The **bell** made **a lot** of **noise**. _____ and _____ made **a lot** of **noise**. Eggbert rolled under the teacher's desk again.

"Come out, Eggbert," said the teacher." Do not be **scared**. It is only the **bell** to **start school**," she said. "Here are many new **friends**. They want to play with you."

All the **children sat** at their desks. They were very, very **quiet**. They wanted to **meet** Eggbert. They wanted to **meet** their new **friend**.

Eggbert rolled out from under the big desk of the teacher. He bounced up and down, up and down so he could see all the **children**. He bounced so **high**, he went right onto the teacher's desk. There, up **high** on the big desk, Eggbert could see all the **children**. All the **children** could see Eggbert, too.

"It's a ball," said _____.

"It's a very **special** ball," said _____, the teacher. This is Eggbert. Eggbert can bounce all by himself."

Eggbert hissed **through** his **valve** to say "Hello."

"Oh, he can make **noises**, too," said _____.

"There is a **snake** inside the ball," said _____.

"No, there is no **snake** inside the ball," said the teacher. "That is Eggbert's way to say 'Hello.' He wants to be your **friend**."

Eggbert bounced off the teacher's desk. He rolled and bounced all around the classroom. He bounced by _____ and by _____. They **patted** him. _____ gave Eggbert a **kiss**. It **tickled**. He **sneezed through** his **valve**. It **sounded** like the **sneeze** of a little **kitten**.

Everyone laughed. _____ and_____, two **boys** who liked to play **a lot**, picked up Eggbert and **threw** him around the classroom. Eggbert liked that. It was fun.

The boys threw Eggbert faster and faster. Eggbert liked to fly around the room, but he did not like it when he **hit** the **wall hard**. It hurt.

"**Ouch**," he hissed when he **hit** the **wall hard**.

"**Sorry**," _____ and _____ said. "We will not do that again."

Eggbert was not **mad** at the **boys**. He did not like to **hit** the **wall hard** because it hurt. After that, the **boys threw** Eggbert more **slowly**. He did not **hit** the **wall** again.

The rest of the day was fun. Eggbert rolled around the classroom. He bounced up to give _____ a ball **kiss**. (What is a ball **kiss** like?) Then he bounced into _____'s **lap**.

"Oh," she said, **surprised**. Are you going to help me with my work?"

Eggbert rolled around in her arms. Eggbert bounced down and rolled up to _____'s desk. He was **working hard**. He did not see Eggbert.

Eggbert hissed a "Hello." He then rolled to the next desk.

_____ picked up Eggbert. "You **need** a **bath**," she told him. "You are a very **dirty** ball. I will carry you into the **bathroom** and wash you."

"What a good **idea**," said the teacher. "I wanted to wash Eggbert today, too. He rolled around **a lot**."

_____ and _____ **took** Eggbert into the **bathroom**. They washed Eggbert in the **sink** with some **smelly soap**. It was green **soap**. Eggbert did not like the green soap, but he did like **getting** clean. Eggbert saw a **funny-looking thing next** to the **sink**. What was it? It was round with a **square tank** at the back. There was **water** in it. What was it? Eggbert did not have **time** to look. Soon he was clean. _____ and _____ put him on the teacher's desk. From the big desk, Eggbert **watched** the class work and play, work and play.

When the class went outside, Eggbert went out, too. _____, _____, _____ _____, and _____ played with Eggbert. They played ball with Eggbert. Outside, there were no **walls** for Eggbert to **hit**.

When the class went inside, Eggbert went in, too. Eggbert was **happy**. When the **bell rang** at the **end** of the day, Eggbert was **surprised**. All the **children left** the classroom. They **waved good-bye** to Eggbert. Eggbert gave the **children** a ball **wave**. (How does a ball **wave** to you?) Eggbert bounced up and down, up and down ten (10) **times**. This is how a ball **waves**. (How do you **wave**? Can you show Eggbert how you **wave**?)

After the **children** went **home** for the day, Eggbert and the teacher said, "**Good-bye**." The teacher said, "**Good-bye**," and Eggbert hissed. Before she went **home**, the teacher **blew** more **air** into Eggbert.

"You're a **special** ball," she said. "My **children love** you. Be a good ball. Go to sleep on my desk, and we will be back **tomorrow**."

That **night**, Eggbert was **lonely** again. He could not sleep. He rolled around the classroom. He bounced onto _____'s desk. The teacher's desk was **messy**. Eggbert rolled into the **bathroom**. It was **dark** inside. The light was off. Eggbert bounced up and up, higher and higher. He bounced right into the **toilet**! It was **wet** and cold. Eggbert could not bounce out of the **toilet**. He could not bounce out of **water**. He **slept** in the **toilet** all **night**. It was wet and cold.

The next morning the teacher and _____, _____, and_____ came to **school early**. They opened the **door** of the classroom. They looked and looked, but they did not see Eggbert.

Where was he? _____ looked in all the **shelves** and **cubbies**. _____ looked under all the desks. The teacher looked up high. It was not funny. Where was Eggbert? Then _____ **heard** a **splash** in the **bathroom**. All three **children** ran into the **bathroom**. There was Eggbert in the **toilet**.

"This is no place for a ball," said _____. She picked Eggbert up from the **toilet** and washed him in the **sink** with the **smelly** green **soap**.

"Ewww," said _____.

The **rest** of the children came into the classroom. Eggbert was **happy** again. He bounced up to give a ball **kiss** to every **boy** and **girl**. All day he bounced and rolled around the classroom.

When the **bell rang** at the **end** of the day, Eggbert did not want to say "**Good-bye**." The children did not want to say "**Good-bye**."

"I have an **idea**," said the kind teacher.

What was the teacher's **idea**? Would Eggbert be **lonely** again? Where could Eggbert sleep every **night**?

"I know what to do," said _____. Eggbert can come **home** with me **tonight**. He can go **home** with _____**tomorrow night**. Who will take Eggbert **home** the **next night**?

That was the teacher's **idea**, too. Every day Eggbert bounced, rolled, read, worked, and played at **school**. Every **night** he went **home** with a **boy** or **girl**. Eggbert was a very **happy** ball.

120 STUDENT CAUGHT'YAS WITH TEACHER'S KEY

CAUGHT'YA VOCABULARY

TEXT TO BE READ ALOUD BY THE TEACHER

bounces♥	toy store♥	arrived	special♥	factory	waiting
shelves♥	flickered	valve♥	Eggbert♥	window♥	
barely	bounced♥	sigh♥	understand	envied	

♥ repeated frequently in the Caught'yas

CAUGHT'YAS

1. sat, inside, outside
2. outside, high
3. bright
4. outside, window, boys, girls
5. people
6. stopped, window, boys, girls
7. boy, girl, whiskers
8. meow, outside, inside
9. wanted, roll, bounce, boys, girls, feel
10. roll, bounce, outside
11. sighed, door, store
12. opened, door, toy store, window
13. back, store, bounced, times, himself
14. sighed, wanted
15. hear, toy store
16. sat, window, dark, outside, night
17. heard, hear, sigh
18. lonely, night, bounced, window, store
19. bounce, roll, night, boys, girls
20. found, floor, back, window, talk
21. found, high, shelf, back, window
22. every, found, window, strange
23. back, window, night, bounced
24. special, bounced, times
25. nice, bounce, himself
26. nice, lady, store, a lot, teacher
27. lady, nice, kind, excited
28. lady, toy, store, back, front
29. sighed, bounced
30. lady, heard, sigh, through, valve
31. lady, buy, special, children, classroom
32. rolled, left, right, joy
33. someone, noticed, talked, could, talk, back
34. sighed, air, through, valve, hiss, snake, lady, excited
35. talk, cried, hiss, snake, roll, else
36. times, lady, rolled, feet, hiss, home
37. lady's, feet, higher, arms
38. lady, cost, hissed, rolled, lady's, arms, tag

39. lady, tag, going, hiss, children
40. paid, took, arms, bag, knew, store
41. car, doors, back, window
42. shelf, window, explained
43. carefully, shelf, window
44. other, cars, road, slowly
45. people, other, window
46. barked, rode, bark, back, hissed
47. bark
48. car, name, waved, back, window, wave
49. times, waves, tried, sounded, hiss
50. air, hiss, flat
51. window, building, school
52. school, live, classroom, shelf
53. doors, front, school, excited
54. excited, hissed, flat, picked, back
55. flat, hissed, fix, blow, air, valve
56. could, flat, poor
57. school, hall, door, a lot, desks
58. classroom, boys, girls, every, love
59. desk, papers, covered, mess, teacher's
60. messy, desk, children, classroom, things, heard, noises
61. picture, classroom
62. a lot, desks, desk, tried, flat
63. lady, need, air, valve, blew
64. fix, blew, air, valve, rolled, tickled
65. papers, paper, sorry, tickle, times
66. talk, snake
67. left, classroom, waved, desk
68. tomorrow, door, closed, quiet, classroom
69. lonely, door, inside, classroom, behind
70. desk, thought, tomorrow
71. teacher's, desk, next, morning, loud, bell, woke, fell
72. bell, rang, rolled, teacher's, desk, still, classroom
73. ready, students
74. everywhere, desks, shelves, bathroom
75. classroom, teacher
76. teacher, surprise
77. teacher
78. everywhere, funny-looking, thing, teacher
79. teacher

80. bell, rang, children, a lot, noise
81. scared, bell, start, school, friends
82. children, sat, quiet, meet, friend
83. children, high
84. high, children
85. special
86. through, valve, noises, snake
87. snake, friend
88. patted
89. kiss, tickled, sneezed, through, valve, sounded, sneeze, kitten
90. boys, a lot, threw
91. hit, wall, hard
92. ouch, hit, wall, hard, sorry
93. mad, boys, hit, wall, hard, threw, slowly
94. kiss
95. lap, surprised
96. working, hard
97. need, bath, dirty, bathroom
98. idea, a lot, took, bathroom
99. sink, smelly, soap, getting
100. funny-looking, thing, next, sink, square, tank, water
101. time, watched
102. walls, hit
103. happy, bell, rang, end, surprised
104. children, left, waved, good-bye, wave
105. times, waves, wave
106. children, home, good-bye, blew, air
107. special, children, love, tomorrow
108. night, lonely
109. messy, bathroom, dark
110. toilet, wet
111. toilet, water, slept, night
112. school, early, door
113. shelves, cubbies
114. heard, splash, bathroom, children
115. toilet, sink, smelly, soap
116. rest, happy, kiss, boy, girl
117. bell, rang, end, good-bye, idea
118. idea, lonely, night
119. home, tonight, tomorrow, night, next
120. idea, school, night, home, boy, girl, happy

Text to Be Read Aloud by the Teacher

Read the following to the class at the beginning of the year to introduce the background of the story. Vocabulary that is way beyond the primary level is in bold type the first time each word is used. Since this part of the story is intended for you to read out loud to the class, the words are bolded only to warn you of their level of difficulty. Words with hearts (♥) after them are repeated frequently in the Caught'yas.

"Eggbert, the Ball, Bounces♥ by Himself"

It was dark in the toy store. It was quiet. Toys sat on long gray **shelves♥**. On the wall, a clock tick-tocked. The clock tick-tocked so softly you could **barely** hear it. The **toy store♥** was closed and locked up for the night.

Suddenly, at the end of one of the rows of shelves, near the far wall of the store, a light **flickered** on and off, on and off like Tinkerbell. There was a sound like a small bell. Something rolled on a shelf and fell to the floor with a small thump.

Whatever it was sat there a minute. Then it **bounced♥**, slowly at first, then faster and faster and higher and higher. It **arrived** at the front of the store. It bounced one more time up into the big front window of the store. There it stopped. It made a noise from the **valve♥** in its side. (*Show a valve and explain its use.*) The noise sounded like a **sigh♥**.

What had bounced all on its own without boy or girl hands to move it? What had sighed? What was in the big window of the toy store? A ball!

This ball was round like all other balls. It did not look much different from all other balls. This ball was... (***Insert your own description of the ball you have in your classroom.***)

But, this was no ordinary ball. This ball was **special♥**. This ball had a name—**Eggbert♥**. This ball could bounce all by itself! This ball could think. This ball even could **understand** people talking! Eggbert was special.

Now, Eggbert did not know how or why he was different from all the other balls. He just was. One minute he had been on the shelf with all the other balls. He did not think. He could not move. Then a light had flickered on and off like Tinkerbell. All of a sudden Eggbert could think. He could move by himself.

Now, Eggbert had rolled and bounced himself to the big front window of the store. He wanted to see what was outside the store. You see, none of the toys knew what was outside the store. They saw the inside of a **factory**. Then they saw the inside of a big brown box. Then they saw the inside of the toy store. No toy in the store had ever been outside in the big world.

This was why the minute Eggbert knew he could bounce all by himself, he bounced his way to the front **window♥**. He had always **envied** the lucky toys who sat in the window. They could see outside.

Eggbert sat the rest of the night in the toy store window. He was **waiting**. He did not know what he was waiting for. But, Eggbert waited anyway...

Stop reading out loud here.

S = Student sentence to correct   **C = Corrected version of the Caught'ya**

> **NOTE:** *You will need to use student names at least fifty-four times in this story. On the day of a Caught'ya that requires student names, put the names on the board so that your students can copy them into their Caught'yas. Or, if you are copying these pages from the CD, insert the names of your students before you run them off.*
>
> *The Caught'yas that require student names (some more than one) are #5, #48, #75, #76, #77, #78, #79, #80, #84, #86, #88, #89, #90, #92, #94, #95, #96, #97, #98, #101, #102, #108, #112, #113, #114, #115, and #119.*

1. sat, inside, outside

PARAGRAPH – beginning of story

CAPITALIZATION – sentences begin with a capital letter; capitalize proper nouns

PUNCTUATION – sentences always have end punctuation

VOWELS – short "a"

VERB TENSE – "sat" is past tense of irregular verb "to sit"; "was" is past tense of irregular verb "to be"

S –   Eggbert **sat** and s___t. It was dark **inside**. It w___s black **outside**.

C –   Eggbert **sat** and **sat**. It was dark **inside**. It w<u>a</u>s black **outside**.

---

2. outside, high

NO PARAGRAPH – continuation of story

CAPITALIZATION – sentences begin with a capital letter

PUNCTUATION – sentences always have end punctuation

COMMAS – need a comma to separate repeated information

VOWELS – short "a"

CONSONANTS – initial "b" sound

VERB TENSE – add "ed" to most verbs to put in past tense; "went" is past tense of irregular verb "to go"; "came" is past tense of irregular verb "to come"

S – The ___lack **outside** went away. The sun came up. It looked like a big ball, a ___ig yellow ___all **high** in the sky.

C – The <u>b</u>lack **outside** went away. The sun came up. It looked like a big ball, a <u>b</u>ig yellow <u>b</u>all **high** in the sky.

3. bright

No PARAGRAPH – same subject

CAPITALIZATION – sentences begin with a capital letter; capitalize proper nouns

PUNCTUATION – sentences always have end punctuation

VOWELS – short "u"

CONSONANTS – "s" sound

VERB TENSE – add "ed" to most verbs to put them in the past tense; "was" is past tense of irregular verb "to be"

S – The ___un wa___ **bright** and pretty. The ___un was big and yellow. Eggbert looked around.

C – The <u>s</u>un wa<u>s</u> **bright** and pretty. The <u>s</u>un was big and yellow. Eggbert looked around.

4. outside, window, boys, girls

No PARAGRAPH – same subject

CAPITALIZATION – sentences begin with a capital letter; capitalize proper nouns

PUNCTUATION – sentences always have end punctuation

VOWELS – "oo" digraph; short "a"

PLURAL RULE – make most nouns plural by adding "s"

VERB TENSE – add "ed" to most verbs to put in past tense; "saw" is past tense of irregular verb "to see"

S – Eggbert looked **outside** the **window**. He l___ ___ked and l___ ___ked. Eggbert saw **boys** and **girls** run by.

C – Eggbert looked **outside** the **window**. He l<u>oo</u>ked and l<u>oo</u>ked. Eggbert saw **boys** and **girls** run by.

5. people

> **NOTE:** *You need to insert the names of three students.*

No PARAGRAPH – same subject

CAPITALIZATION – sentences begin with a capital letter; capitalize proper nouns

PUNCTUATION – sentences always have end punctuation

COMMAS – needed between 2 adjectives where 2nd adj. is not age, size, color, or linked to noun

VOWELS – short "e"; short "a"

VERB TENSE – "went" is past tense of irregular verb "to go"; "saw" is past tense of irregular verb "to see"

OTHER SKILLS – name recognition

S – Big, tall **people** went by. Short, f___t **people** w___nt by. _____ and _____ _ and _____ r___n by. No one s___w Eggbert.

C – Big, tall **people** went by. Short, f<u>a</u>t **people** w<u>e</u>nt by. _____ and _____ and _____ r<u>a</u>n by. No one s<u>a</u>w Eggbert.

6. stopped, window, boys, girls

No paragraph – same subject

Capitalization – sentences begin with a capital letter; capitalize proper nouns

Punctuation – sentences always have end punctuation

Vowels – "oo" digraph; short "a"

Plural rule – add "s" to most nouns

Verb tense – add "ed" to most verbs to put in past tense; "saw" is past tense of irregular verb "to see"

Spelling rule – note the double "p" in "stopped" (consonant/vowel/consonant + suffix = consonant must be doubled)

Literary device – repeating words

S – No one **stopped** to look in the **window**. Eggbert looked and l___ ___ked. He saw **boys** and **girls**. He s___ ___ dogs and c___ts.

C – No one **stopped** to look in the **window**. Eggbert looked and l<u>oo</u>ked. He saw **boys** and **girls**. He s<u>a</u>w dogs and c<u>a</u>ts.

---

7. boy, girl, whiskers

No paragraph – same subject

Capitalization – sentences begin with a capital letter; capitalize proper nouns

Punctuation – sentences always have end punctuation

Vowels – short "a"; "oo" digraph in middle of word

Plural rules – add "s" to most nouns

Verb tense – add "ed" to most verbs to put in past tense; "ran" is past tense of irregular verb "to run"

Literary device – alliteration ("white whiskers")

S – A **boy** ran by. A **girl** r___n by. A big dog r___ ___ by. A bl___ck and white c___t with long white **whiskers** l___ ___ked at Eggbert.

C – A **boy** ran by. A **girl** r<u>a</u>n by. A big dog r<u>a</u>n by. A bl<u>a</u>ck and white c<u>a</u>t with long white **whiskers** l<u>oo</u>ked at Eggbert.

---

8. meow, outside, inside

No paragraph – same subject

Capitalization – sentences begin with a capital letter; capitalize proper nouns

Punctuation – sentences always have end punctuation; quotation marks around what is said out loud

Comma – quote

Vowels – short "a"; "ou" blend

Verb tense – "said" is past tense of irregular verb "to say"; "was" is past tense of irregular verb "to be"

Literary device – onomatopoeia (a word that imitates a sound)

S – It said, "**Meow.**" The c___t was **outside**. Eggbert w___s not ___ ___tside. He w___s **inside**.

C – It said, "**Meow.**" The c<u>a</u>t was **outside**. Eggbert w<u>a</u>s not **<u>ou</u>tside**. He w<u>a</u>s **inside**.

9. wanted, roll, bounce, boys, girls, feel

PARAGRAPH – new idea
CAPITALIZATION – sentences begin with a capital letter; capitalize proper nouns
PUNCTUATION – sentences always have end punctuation
VOWELS – short "e"
PLURAL RULE – add "s" to most nouns
VERB TENSE – add "ed" to most verbs to put in past tense

S –   Eggbert **wanted** to **roll** and **bounce** with the **boys** and **girls**. He **want___d** to go with th___m. He **wanted** to **feel** th___ sun.

C –   Eggbert **wanted** to **roll** and **bounce** with the **boys** and **girls**. He **wanted** to go with th<u>em</u>. He **wanted** to **feel** th<u>e</u> sun.

---

10. roll, bounce, outside

PARAGRAPH – new person speaking
CAPITALIZATION – sentences begin with a capital letter; capitalize proper nouns; always capitalize "I"
PUNCTUATION – sentences always have end punctuation; note use of quotation marks around what is said out loud
VOWELS – short "e" in "em"; short "a" in "an"
VERB TENSE – change to present tense in quote; "said" is past tense of irregular verb "to say"

S –   "I w___nt to be with them," Eggbert said. "I w___ ___t to **roll** and **bounce** with th___ ___.
I
w___ ___ ___ to see the **outside**."

C –   "I w<u>a</u>nt to be with them," Eggbert said. "I w<u>a</u>nt to **roll** and **bounce** with th<u>em</u>. I w<u>a</u>nt to see the **outside**."

---

11. sighed, door, store

PARAGRAPH – new person speaking (narrator)
CAPITALIZATION – sentences begin with a capital letter; capitalize proper nouns
PUNCTUATION – sentences always have end punctuation
VOWELS – long "i" in "igh"; long "a" with silent "e"
VERB TENSE – add "ed" to most verbs to put in past tense
Literary device – rhyme

S –   Eggbert **sighed**. He s___gh___d and s___ ___ ___ed. Then a tall man c___me to the **door** of the **store**.

C –   Eggbert **sighed**. He s<u>igh</u>ed and s<u>igh</u>ed. Then a tall man c<u>a</u>me to the **door** of the **store**.

12. opened, door, toy store, window

No paragraph – same subject, referring to same person
Capitalization – sentences begin with a capital letter
Punctuation – sentences always have end punctuation
Vowels – short "a" in "all"; short "o"; short "i"; long "a"
Verb tense – add "ed" to most verbs to put in past tense; "came" is past tense of irregular verb "to come"
Literary device – rhyme

S – The t___ ___ ___ man **opened** the **door**. He c___me in the **toy store**. He did n___t see Eggbert in the b___g **window**.

C – The t<u>a</u>ll man **opened** the **door**. He c<u>a</u>me in the **toy store**. He did n<u>o</u>t see Eggbert in the b<u>i</u>g **window**.

---

13. back, store, bounced, times, himself

No paragraph – same subject, same speaker
Capitalization – sentences begin with a capital letter; capitalize proper nouns
Punctuation – sentences always have end punctuation
Commas – need a comma to separate repeated information ("up and down")
Vowels – "ow" sound in "down"; short "u"; double long "e"; short "a," "e," and "o"; long "e" when vowel is repeated; "ou" digraph
Plural rule – add "s" to most nouns (times)
Verb tense – add "ed" to most verbs to put in past tense
Other skill – reflexive pronouns (himself)

S – The man w___nt to the **back** of the **store**. Eggbert saw him look around. Eggbert **bounced** up and down, ___p and down, up and d___ ___ ___ thr___ ___ (3) **times**. The m___n did n___t se___ Eggbert bounce by **himself**.

C – The man w<u>e</u>nt to the **back** of the **store**. Eggbert saw him look around. Eggbert **bounced** up and down, <u>up</u> and down, up and d<u>own</u> three (3) **times**. The m<u>a</u>n did n<u>o</u>t se<u>e</u> Eggbert bounce by **himself**.

14. sighed, wanted

No paragraph – same subject, same speaker
Capitalization – sentences begin with a capital letter; capitalize proper nouns
Punctuation – sentences always have end punctuation
Vowels – short "a" and "i"; long "i"
Verb tense – add "ed" to most verbs to put in past tense
Other skill – learning how to spell name

S – Eggbert **sighed** and s___ ___ ___ed. He **wanted** the man to see him. The man did not see him. The man d___d not see E___ ___ ___ ___ ___t.

C – Eggbert **sighed** and **sighed**. He **wanted** the man to see him. The man did not see him. The man d_i_d not see _Eggbert_.

---

15. hear, toy store

No paragraph – same subject, referring to same person
Capitalization – sentences begin with a capital letter; capitalize proper nouns
Punctuation – sentences always have end punctuation
Vowels – "or" sound; review of short vowel sounds
Verb tense – add "ed" to most verbs to put in past tense; "was" is past tense of the irregular verb "to be"
Prepositions – You might want to find a list of prepositions (see the **Grammar, Usage, and Mechanics Guide**) and begin to have your students memorize them. This is a useful tool; preposition "in" in this Caught'ya

S – The man did n___t **hear** Eggbert. The man w___rked in the **toy store**. He liked to w___rk in the **toy st___ ___e**. It was f___n.

C – The man did n_o_t **hear** Eggbert. The man w_o_rked in the **toy store**. He liked to w_o_rk in the **toy st_o_re**. It was f_u_n.

---

16. sat, window, dark, outside, night

Paragraph – change of topic and person
Capitalization – sentences begin with a capital letter
Punctuation – sentences always have end punctuation
Vowels – review of short vowel sounds
Verb tense – add "ed" to most verbs to put in past tense; "sat" is past tense of irregular verb "to sit"; "got" is past tense of irregular verb "to get"
Prepositions – review and learn (outside, in)

S –   Eggbert **sat** in the **window** all day. Then it g___t **dark outside**. Eggbert s___t in the w___ndow all **night**.

C –   Eggbert **sat** in the **window** all day. Then it g_o_t **dark outside**. Eggbert s_a_t in the w_i_ndow all **night**.

17. heard, hear, sigh

NO PARAGRAPH – same subject, same speaker
CAPITALIZATION – sentences begin with a capital letter; capitalize proper nouns
PUNCTUATION – sentences always have end punctuation; note question needs end punctuation of
    question mark
VOWELS – "oo" digraph; short vowel review
VERB TENSE – add "ed" to most verbs to put in past tense
SPELLING RULE – "no one" is 2 words
OTHER SKILLS – name recognition; homophones ("hear/here")

S – No one saw Eggbert. No one **heard** E___ ___ ___ ___ ___t. Only a black and white cat
    look___d at Eggb___ ___t. Can you **hear** a b___ ___ ___ **sigh**?

C – No one saw Eggbert. No one **heard** Egg<u>b</u>ert. Only a black and white cat look<u>e</u>d at Egg<u>b</u>ert.
    Can you **hear** a b<u>all</u> **sigh**?

---

18. lonely, night, bounced, window, store

PARAGRAPH – change of topic
CAPITALIZATION – sentences begin with a capital letter; capitalize proper nouns
PUNCTUATION – sentences always have end punctuation
VOWELS – short "a"; long "o" when followed by consonant/silent "e"
VERB TENSE – add "ed" to most verbs to put in past tense; "was" is past tense of irregular verb "to be"
PREPOSITIONS – review and continue to learn (out, of, into)

S –   Eggbert w___s very sad. Eggbert w___ ___ very **lonely**. One **night** he **bounced** out of the
    window into the **store**.

C –   Eggbert w<u>a</u>s very sad. Eggbert w<u>as</u> very **lonely**. One **night** he **bounced** out of the **window**
    into the **store**.

---

19. bounce, roll, night, boys, girls

PARAGRAPH – new speaker
CAPITALIZATION – sentences begin with a capital letter; capitalize proper nouns; always capitalize "I"
PUNCTUATION – sentences always have end punctuation; note use of quotation marks around what is
    said out loud
COMMA – quote
VOWELS – final "e" in two-letter word = long "e"; double "e" = long "e"
PLURAL RULE – add "s" to most nouns
VERB TENSE – future tense with "will"; "said" is past tense of irregular verb "to say"

S –   "I will **bounce** and **roll**," Eggbert said one **night**. "The man will see m___. **Boys** and **girls**
    will s___ ___ me."

C –   "I will **bounce** and **roll**," Eggbert said one **night**. "The man will see m<u>e</u>. **Boys** and **girls**
    will s<u>ee</u> me."

20. found, floor, back, window, talk

PARAGRAPH – different topic; refers to different person
CAPITALIZATION – sentences begin with a capital letter; capitalize proper nouns
PUNCTUATION – sentences always have end punctuation
VOWELS – long "a" if followed by "y"; review of short vowels
CONSONANTS – "lk" sound
VERB TENSE – add "ed" to most verbs to put in past tense
OTHER SKILL – name recognition

S –   One d___y the m___n **found** Eggbert on the **floor**. He p___t Eggbert **back** in the **window**. He d___d n___t **talk** to Egg___ ___ ___t.

C –   One day the man **found** Eggbert on the **floor**. He put Eggbert **back** in the **window**. He did not **talk** to Eggbert.

21. found, high, shelf, back, window

NO PARAGRAPH – same topic; same person
CAPITALIZATION – sentences begin with a capital letter; capitalize proper nouns
PUNCTUATION – sentences always have end punctuation
VOWELS – short "a"; short "u"
VERB TENSE – "found" is past tense of irregular verb "to find"; "put" is past tense of irregular verb "to put"
PREPOSITIONS – review and continue to learn (up, on, in)
OTHER SKILL – name recognition

S – One day the man **found** E___ ___bert **high** ___p on a **shelf**. He p___t Eggbert **back** in the **window**.

C – One day the man **found** Eggbert **high** up on a **shelf**. He put Eggbert **back** in the **window**.

22. every, found, window, strange

PARAGRAPH – change of time
CAPITALIZATION – sentences begin with a capital letter; capitalize proper nouns
PUNCTUATION – sentences always have end punctuation; use of exclamation mark for emphasis; question mark needed at end of question
VOWELS – short vowel review; long vowel with silent "e" at end of word
VERB TENSE – "found" is past tense of irregular verb "to find"; "came" is past tense of irregular verb "to come"; use of "would" as conditional
LITERARY DEVICE – deliberate use of fragment ("What a strange ball!)

S –   **Every** day the man **found** Eggbert out of the **window**. What a **strange** b___ll! Where would the b___ ___ ___ be **every** day wh___n the m___n c___me to w___rk?

C –   **Every** day the man **found** Eggbert out of the **window**. What a **strange** ball! Where would the ball be **every** day when the man came to work?

23. back, window, night, bounced

NO PARAGRAPH – same topic

CAPITALIZATION – sentences begin with a capital letter; capitalize proper nouns

PUNCTUATION – sentences always have end punctuation

VOWELS – "ow" sound and how it varies

VERB TENSE – add "ed" to most verbs to put in past tense; "put" is past tense of irregular verb "to put"

PREPOSITIONS – review and continue to learn (in, out, of)

OTHER SKILLS – word recognition

S – Every day the man put Eggbert **back** in the **window**. Ev__ __ __ **night** Eggbert **bounced** out of the **w**__ __ __ __**w**.

C – Every day the man put Eggbert **back** in the **window**. Ev<u>ery</u> **night** Eggbert **bounced** out of the **w**<u>indo</u>**w**.

---

24. special, bounced, times

2 PARAGRAPHS – new person speaking; topic change

CAPITALIZATION – sentences begin with a capital letter; capitalize proper nouns

PUNCTUATION – sentences always have end punctuation; note use of quotation marks around what is said aloud

COMMAS – quote; repetition

VOWELS – other "ow" sound; double "e" as long "e"

VERB TENSE – switch to present tense in quote; "said" is past tense of irregular verb "to say"; add "ed" to most verbs to put in past tense

PREPOSITIONS – review and continue to learn (up, down)

S – "This ball is **special**," the man said.
Eggbert **bounced** up and down, up and d<u>__ __ __</u>, up and d<u>__ __ __</u> thr<u>__ __</u> (3) **times** to say "Yes."

C – "This ball is **special**," the man said.
Eggbert **bounced** up and down, up and d<u>own</u>, up and d<u>own</u> thr<u>ee</u> (3) **times** to say "Yes."

---

25. nice, bounce, himself

NO PARAGRAPH – same subject

CAPITALIZATION – sentences begin with a capital letter; capitalize proper nouns

PUNCTUATION – sentences always have end punctuation; note question mark at end of question

VOWELS – review short vowel sounds

VERB TENSE – add "ed" to most verbs to put in past tense; "was" is past tense of irregular verb "to be"

PREPOSITIONS – review and continue to learn (by)

LITERARY DEVICE – note deliberate use of fragment in narrator aside ("No")

OTHER SKILL – name recognition

S – Did the **nice** m__n see Eggbert **bounce** by **himself**? No. Egg__ __ __ t w__s s__d.

C – Did the **nice** m<u>a</u>n see Eggbert **bounce** by **himself**? No. Egg<u>bert</u> w<u>as</u> s<u>a</u>d.

26. nice, lady, store, a lot, teacher

PARAGRAPH – change of topic
CAPITALIZATION – sentences begin with a capital letter; capitalize proper nouns
PUNCTUATION – sentences always have end punctuation; need question mark after question
VOWELS – silent "e" at end of word renders vowels long
VERB TENSE – "came" is past tense of irregular verb "to come"; add "ed" to most verbs to put in past tense; "was" is past tense of irregular verb "to be"

S –   One day a **nice lady** c___m___ in the **store**. She looked **a lot** l___k___ your **teacher**. Who was she? What did she want?

C –   One day a **nice lady** c<u>a</u>m<u>e</u> in the **store**. She looked **a lot** l<u>ike</u> your **teacher**. Who was she? What did she want?

27. lady, nice, kind, excited

NO PARAGRAPH – same topic; same speaker
CAPITALIZATION – sentences begin with a capital letter; capitalize proper nouns
PUNCTUATION – sentences always have end punctuation
VOWELS – short "a"; long "i" when followed by consonant/silent "e"
VERB TENSE – add "ed" to most verbs to put in past tense; "was" is past tense of irregular verb "to be"
OTHER SKILL – word recognition

S – This **lady** looked **n___ ___ ___**. She l___ ___ ___ ___ ___ **kind**. Eggbert w___ ___ **excited**.

C – This **lady** looked **n<u>ice</u>**. She <u>looked</u> **kind**. Eggbert w<u>as</u> **excited**.

28. lady, toy store, back, front

NO PARAGRAPH – same topic; same speaker
CAPITALIZATION – sentences begin with a capital letter; capitalize proper nouns
PUNCTUATION – sentences always have end punctuation
VOWELS – "oo" digraph; "ou" blend
VERB TENSE – add "ed" to most verbs to put in past tense
PREPOSITIONS – review and continue to learn (around, in, of)
OTHER SKILL – word practice

S – The **lady** l___ ___ked ar___ ___nd the **toy store**. She l___ ___ ___ed in the **back** of the **store**. She l___ ___ked in the **front** of the **store**.

C – The **lady** l<u>oo</u>ked ar<u>ou</u>nd the **toy store**. She <u>looked</u> in the **back** of the **store**. She <u>looked</u> in the **front** of the **store**.

29. sighed, bounced

PARAGRAPH – new speaker
CAPITALIZATION – sentences begin with a capital letter; capitalize proper nouns
PUNCTUATION – sentences always have end punctuation; note quotes around what is said out loud
COMMA – quote
VOWELS – long "i" with "gh"; "ow" sound; review long vowel rules
VERB TENSE – add "ed" to most verbs to put in past tense; switch to present tense for quote
PREPOSITIONS – review and continue to learn (up, down, with)

S –   Eggbert **sighed** and s___ ___ ___ ed. He **bounced** up and d___ ___n. "Please see me.
    Pl___ ___se s___ ___ me," he wanted to say. "Please take m___ with you. Pl___ ___se t___ ___
    ___ me with you."

C –   Eggbert **sighed** and **sighed**. He **bounced** up and d<u>ow</u>n. "Please see me. Pl<u>ea</u>se s<u>ee</u> me,"
    he wanted to say. "Please take m<u>e</u> with you. Pl<u>ea</u>se t<u>a</u>ke me with you."

> **NOTE:** *For the next ten Caught'yas, some of the sentences are missing capitalization. This has been done to make it easy for you if you feel your students can put in the capital letters by themselves. If not, you can simply pen in the missing capital letters before you copy the sentences from the CD.*

30. lady, heard, sigh, through, valve

PARAGRAPH – change of topic
CAPITALIZATION – sentences begin with a capital letter; capitalize proper nouns
PUNCTUATION – sentences always have end punctuation
VOWELS – "ow" sound; "ou" digraph"; "ea" digraph;
VERB TENSE – "saw" is past tense of irregular verb "to see"; "heard" is past tense of irregular verb "to hear"
PREPOSITIONS – review and continue to learn (up, down, through)
OTHER SKILLS – name recognition, introduce sense verbs

S –   The **lady** saw E___ ___ ___ ___ ___t. she saw him b___ ___nce up and d___ ___n. She
    heard him **sigh through** his **valve**.

C –   The **lady** saw E<u>ggb</u>ert. She saw him b<u>ou</u>nce up and d<u>ow</u>n. She **heard** him **sigh through**
    his **valve**.

31. lady, buy, special, children, classroom

PARAGRAPH – new speaker
CAPITALIZATION – sentences begin with a capital letter; capitalize proper nouns; always capitalize "I"
PUNCTUATION – sentences always have end punctuation; note quotes around what is said out loud; note use of exclamation mark for emphasis
COMMAS – quote
VOWELS – "ai" and "ei" digraphs; "ou" digraph
VERB TENSE – add "ed" to most verbs to put in past tense; "was" is past tense of irregular verb "to be"; switch to present tense for quote
PREPOSITIONS – review and continue to learn (to, at, in)
OTHER SKILLS – name recognition; learn homophones "their" as possessive pronoun

S –   the **lady** said to the man in the store, "I want to **buy** this ball. this ball is **special**. To Eggbert she s___ ___d, "How my **children** at _____ would like to have y___ ___ in th___ ___r **classroom**!"

C –   The **lady** said to the man in the store, "I want to **buy** this ball. This ball is **special**. To Eggbert she s<u>ai</u>d, "How my **children** at (*put your school name here*) would like to have y<u>ou</u> in th<u>ei</u>r **classroom**!"

---

32. rolled, left, right, joy

PARAGRAPH – change of topic
CAPITALIZATION – sentences begin with a capital letter; capitalize proper nouns
PUNCTUATION – sentences always have end punctuation
VOWELS – "ow" sound
CONSONANTS – "ll" sound in "rolled" and "full"
VERB TENSE – add "ed" to most verbs to put in past tense; "was" is past tense of irregular verb "to be"
PREPOSITIONS – review and continue to learn (to, of)
OTHER SKILL – go over "left" and "right"

S –   Eggbert **rolled** up and d___ ___n. he r___ ___ ___ed to the **left** and then to the **right**. He was happy. he was fu___ ___ of **joy**.

C –   Eggbert **rolled** up and d<u>ow</u>n. He **ro<u>ll</u>ed** to the **left** and then to the **right**. He was happy. He was fu<u>ll</u> of **joy**.

33. someone, noticed, talked, could, talk, back

No paragraph – same topic; same speaker
Capitalization – sentences begin with a capital letter; capitalize proper nouns
Punctuation – sentences always have end punctuation; need for question mark after question
Vowels – short "a" and "i"
Consonants – "lk" sound; double consonants; "w"; "sh" blend
Verb tense – add "ed" to most verbs to put in past tense; "was" is past tense of irregular verb "to be"; switch to present tense for quote; "could" as conditional ("maybe") tense needed after "if"

S – why was E___ ___bert ha___ ___y? **Someone noticed** him. **someone talked** to h___m. Eggbert wi___ ___ed he **could talk back**.

C – Why was Eggbert happy? **Someone noticed** him. Someone **talked** to him. Eggbert wished he **could talk back**.

---

34. sighed, air, through, valve, hiss, snake, lady, excited

> **NOTE:** *Since this Caught'ya has so many vocabulary words (although many are repeats), you may want to use this as a vocabulary lesson.*

Paragraph – change of idea
Capitalization – sentences begin with a capital letter; capitalize proper nouns
Punctuation – sentences always have end punctuation
Comma – comma in a compound sentence (see **Grammar, Usage, and Mechanics Guide**)
Vowels – review of short vowels and long vowels
Consonants – "th" blend
Verb tense – add "ed" to most verbs to put in past tense; "was" is past tense of irregular verb "to be"; "heard" is past tense of irregular verb "to hear"
Prepositions – review and continue to learn (through, with)
Literary device –simile

S –   eggbert s___ghed. He let **air** come **through** h___s **valve** wi___ ___ a **hiss** l___ke a **snake**. the **lady** heard him, and she was very **excited**.

C –   Eggbert **sighed**. He let **air** come **through** his **valve** with a **hiss** like a **snake**. The **lady** heard him, and she was very **excited**.

35. talk, cried, hiss, snake, roll, else

PARAGRAPH – new person speaking
CAPITALIZATION – sentences begin with a capital letter; capitalize proper nouns
PUNCTUATION – sentences always have end punctuation; note quotes around what is said out loud;
    question needs question mark at end (note placement in quotation)
COMMAS – after interjection ("Oh"); compound sentence
VOWELS – "ou" digraph; "ou" blend; "o" at end of word as "ooooo" sound
CONSONANTS – "lk"; double consonant sounds
VERB TENSE – add "ed" to most verbs to put in past tense; "was" is past tense of irregular verb "to be";
    switch to present tense for quote
PREPOSITIONS – review and continue to learn (with, by)
OTHER SKILL – reflexive pronouns (myself, yourself, etc.)
LITERARY DEVICE – simile

S –   "Oh, y___ ___ **talk**," she **cried** ___ ___t with joy. "you **hiss** like a **snake**, and y___ ___
    b___ ___nce and **roll** all by y___ ___rself. What **else** can you d___?" she asked Eggbert.

C –   "Oh, y<u>ou</u> **talk**," she **cried** <u>out</u> with joy. "You **hiss** like a **snake**, and y<u>ou</u> b<u>ou</u>nce and **roll** all
    by y<u>our</u>self. What **else** can you d<u>o</u>?" she asked Eggbert.

---

36. times, lady, rolled, feet, hiss, home

PARAGRAPH – new speaker (narrator)
CAPITALIZATION – sentences begin with a capital letter; capitalize proper nouns
PUNCTUATION – sentences always have end punctuation
COMMAS – verb series
VOWELS – "ou" blend; "o" at end of word as "ooooo" sound
CONSONANTS – double "l" sound
VERB TENSE – add "ed" to most verbs to put in past tense
PREPOSITIONS – review and continue to learn (up, onto, out, with)
OTHER SKILL – name recognition

S –   Eggbert bounced five **times**. he b___ ___nced right up to the kind **lady**, r___lled onto her
    feet, and let ___ ___t a **hiss**. ___ ___ ___ ___ ___ ___t wanted the **lady** t___ take him **home**
    with her.

C –   Eggbert bounced five **times**. He b<u>ou</u>nced right up to the kind **lady**, **r<u>o</u>lled** onto her **feet**,
    and let <u>out</u> a **hiss**. <u>Eggbert</u> wanted the **lady** t<u>o</u> take him **home** with her.

37. lady's, feet, higher, arms

No paragraph – same topic; same speaker
Capitalization – sentences begin with a capital letter; capitalize proper nouns
Punctuation – sentences always have end punctuation
Commas – extra information
Vowels – "ou" blend; short "u"
Verb tense – add "ed" to most verbs to put in past tense
Other skills – possessive of singular noun; introduce parts of the body

S – eggbert bounced again, right on the **lady's feet**. Then he b__ __ __ __ __ __ two times, even **higher**. on the next bounce, Eggbert j__mped into the nice **lady's arms**.

C – Eggbert bounced again, right on the **lady's feet**. Then he b<u>ounced</u> two times, even **higher**. On the next bounce, Eggbert j<u>u</u>mped into the nice **lady's arms**.

---

38. lady, cost, hissed, rolled, lady's, arms, tag

2 Paragraphs – new speaker; change to narrator
Capitalization – sentences begin with a capital letter; capitalize proper nouns; always capitalize "I"
Punctuation – sentences always have end punctuation; note quotes around what is said out loud; question mark needed at end of question
Comma – quote
Vowels – "ai,"digraph; "ou" blend; "ou" digraph
Verb tense – "said" is past tense of irregular verb "to say"; add "ed" to most verbs to put in past tense; switch to present tense for quote

S – "oh," s__ __d the **lady** to Eggbert. "I want to buy you. how much do you **cost**?" Eggbert **hissed**. he **rolled** ar__ __nd in the **lady's arms** so she c__ __ld see his **tag**.

C – "Oh," s<u>ai</u>d the **lady** to Eggbert. "I want to buy you. How much do you **cost**?" Eggbert **hissed**. He **rolled** ar<u>ou</u>nd in the **lady's arms** so she c<u>ou</u>ld see his **tag**.

39. lady, tag, going, hiss, children

> **NOTE:** *Put your name on the board so that students can copy it in the blanks in Caught'yas #39, #40, #41, #47, #50, #51, #52, #54, #55, #57, #60, #64, #74, #76, and #85. Or, if you are blowing these up or typing a new copy, insert your name before running off copies for your students.*

PARAGRAPH – new speaker

CAPITALIZATION – sentences begin with a capital letter; capitalize proper nouns

PUNCTUATION – sentences always have end punctuation; note quotes around what is said out loud

COMMAS – quote; series of verbs

VOWELS – long "i" with "gh"; short "e" review

VERB TENSE – switch to present tense for quote

OTHER SKILLS – name recognition; abbreviation in your name

S –   "your name is Eggb___rt," said the **lady**. "It says so right on your **tag**. "h___llo,

___ ___ ___ ___ ___ ___t. My name is _____. you are **going** to laugh, **hiss**,

and play with my **children**."

C –   "Your name is Eggbert," said the **lady**. "It says so right on your **tag**. "Hello, Eggbert. My

name is (***put your name here***). You are **going** to laugh, **hiss**, and play with my **children**."

> **NOTE 1:** *After this point in the student Caught'yas, no sentence has a capital letter at its beginning. If your students are not yet ready to put in the capital letter on their own, simply include it in on the student copy before you run it off from the CD for your class. In addition, prepositions no longer will be pointed out. You might want to have your students recite them as they occur.*
>
> **NOTE 2:** *It is important to target the use of strong, active verbs in children's writing at a very early age. Practice and awareness at age six becomes habit at age eight. From this point on, the use of strong, active verbs will be noted. "Dead" or weak verbs are the following: am, are, be, had, has, have, is, was, were, any verb ending in "ing," and the sense verbs which substitute as verbs of being (see, hear, smell, taste, feel). Strong verbs are all other verbs! Sadly, though, most children use only the "dead" verbs in their writing. The use of strong, active verbs immediately improves any story or essay. After practice, first-graders can produce some really good work using active verbs.*

40. paid, took, arms, bag, knew, store

PARAGRAPH – change of place
CAPITALIZATION – sentences begin with a capital letter; capitalize proper nouns
PUNCTUATION – sentences always have end punctuation
VOWELS – long and short vowel review
VERB TENSE – add "ed" to most verbs to put in past tense; "was" is past tense of irregular verb "to be"
PREPOSITIONS – review and continue to learn (for, outside, in)
OTHER SKILLS – abbreviation in your name; name recognition;

S – _____ **paid** for Eggbert and **took** h___m outs___de ___n her **arms**. she d___d not put eggbert in a **bag**. she **knew** he wanted to see outs___de the **store**.

C – (***Put your name here***) **paid** for Eggbert and **took** him outside in her **arms**. She did not put Eggbert in a **bag**. She **knew** he wanted to see outside the **store**.

---

41. car, doors, back, window

> **NOTE:** *It is good to have your students memorize the coordinating conjunctions: for, and, nor, but, or, yet, so. Once these are memorized, students can learn not to capitalize them in a title, not to begin a sentence with one, and to put a comma before one if there is a complete sentence on either side (a compound sentence).*

NO PARAGRAPH – same topic
CAPITALIZATION – sentences begin with a capital letter; capitalize proper nouns
PUNCTUATION – sentences always have end punctuation
COMMA – compound sentence (see ***Grammar, Usage, and Mechanics Guide***)
VOWELS – short and long vowel review
CONSONANTS – go over consonant blends ("nt," "st," "th," "gr," "ld"); review double consonants
VERB TENSE – "went" is past tense for irregular verb "to go"; "got" is past tense for irregular verb "to get"
OTHER SKILLS – abbreviation in your name; name recognition; color recognition; strong verb use

S – _____ and Eggbert we___ ___ out of the toy ___ ___ore, and ___ ___ey got into a li___ ___le ye___ ___ow **car** with ___ ___een **doors**. _____ put E___ ___bert in the **back** so that he cou___ ___ see out ___ ___e big **back window**.

C – (***Put your name here***) and Eggbert went out of the toy store, and they got into a little yellow **car** with green **doors**. (***Put your name here***) put Eggbert in the **back** so that he could see out the big **back window**.

42. shelf, window, explained

PARAGRAPH – new speaker
CAPITALIZATION – sentences begin with a capital letter; capitalize proper nouns
PUNCTUATION – sentences always have end punctuation; quotes around what is said out loud
COMMAS – quote; long introductory adverb (subordinate clause)
VOWELS – "ai" digraph; "ow" sound as long "o"
CONSONANTS – double consonant sounds like "ll"
VERB TENSE – switch to present tense for quote; add "ed" to most verbs to put in past tense
OTHER SKILL – word recognition

S –   "just don't roll off of the **shelf**," s___ ___d the lady to eggbert. "if you ro___ ___ off the **shelf**, you won't be able to see out the **w__ __ __ __w**," she **explained**.

C –   "Just don't roll off of the **shelf**," s<u>ai</u>d the lady to Eggbert. "If you ro<u>ll</u> off the **shelf**, you won't be able to see out the **w<u>indo</u>w**," she **explained**.

---

43. carefully, shelf, window

PARAGRAPH – new speaker (narrator)
CAPITALIZATION – sentences begin with a capital letter; capitalize proper nouns
PUNCTUATION – sentences always have end punctuation; quotes around what is said out loud
COMMA – quote
CONSONANTS – review; plosive "t" sound; consonant blends; double consonants
VERB TENSE – add "ed" to most verbs to put in past tense; "had" is past tense of irregular verb "to have"
OTHER SKILLS – strong verb
LITERARY DEVICE – use of italics for emphasis

S –   e___ ___ber___ bounced ___ ___ree (3) li___ ___le bounces to ___ay, "Yes." he bou___ ___ ___ ___ very **carefu___ ___y**. he did not wa___ ___ to fall off this **shelf**. *this* s___ ___ ___f had a **window** to the ou___ ___ide.

C –   Egg<u>ber</u>t bounced <u>three</u> li<u>ttle</u> bounces to <u>say</u>, "Yes." He bou<u>nced</u> very **carefully**. He did not wa<u>nt</u> to fall off this **shelf**. *This* s<u>helf</u> had a **window** to the ou<u>tside</u>.

44. other, cars, road, slowly

PARAGRAPH – new topic
CAPITALIZATION – sentences begin with a capital letter; capitalize proper nouns
PUNCTUATION – sentences always have end punctuation
VOWELS – diphthong "oo"; long "i" with silent "e"; short "e"
CONSONANTS – practice "k," "d," and "nt"
VERB TENSE – add "ed "to most verbs to put in past tense; "went" is past tense of irregular verb "to go"
OTHER SKILLS – word recognition; strong verb use

S –   eggbert looked and loo___ ___ ___. he saw **other cars** r___de down the **road**. some went very fast. some w___ ___ ___ very **slowly**.

C –   Eggbert looked and loo<u>ked</u>. He saw **other cars** r<u>i</u>de down the **road**. Some went very fast. Some w<u>ent</u> very **slowly**.

45. people, other, window

NO PARAGRAPH – same topic
CAPITALIZATION – sentences begin with a capital letter; capitalize proper nouns
PUNCTUATION – sentences always have end punctuation
VOWELS – short vowel review
CONSONANTS – initial "b," "c," "d," and "p" sounds
VERB TENSE – add "ed" to most verbs to put in past tense
OTHER SKILL – strong verb use

S –   eggbert liked the slow cars b___st. he could see **people** and dogs inside them. he d___d n___t see **other** b___lls. a big brown d___g in a big blue car p___t its head out the **window**.

C –   Eggbert liked the slow cars b<u>e</u>st. He could see **people** and dogs inside them. He d<u>i</u>d n<u>o</u>t see **other** b<u>a</u>lls. A big brown d<u>o</u>g in a big blue car p<u>u</u>t its head out the **window**.

46. barked, rode, bark, back, hissed

NO PARAGRAPH – same topic; 2 Paragraphs – new persons speaking
CAPITALIZATION – sentences begin with a capital letter; capitalize proper nouns
PUNCTUATION – sentences always have end punctuation; quotes around what is said out loud
COMMAS – quote; compound sentence; compound sentence
CONSONANTS – initial "b," "c," and "d" sounds
VERB TENSE – add "ed" to most verbs to put in past tense; "rode" is past tense of irregular verb "to ride"; "said" is past tense of irregular verb "to say"
OTHER SKILLS – word practice; strong verb use
LITERARY DEVICE – onomatopoeia (a word that imitates a sound); alliteration ("bark back")

S – it **barked** at eggbert as he **rode** by.
     "**bark**. b___ ___k," the dog s___ ___d.
     eggbert w___ ___ted to **bark back** at the dog. he b___ ___ ___ced, and he **hissed**, but he could not **b___ ___k**.

C – It **barked** at Eggbert as he **rode** by.
     "**Bark**. B̲a̲rk," the dog sa̲i̲d.
     Eggbert wa̲nted to **bark back** at the dog. He bo̲u̲nced, and he **hissed**, but he could not **bark**.

---

47. bark

PARAGRAPH – new persons peaking
CAPITALIZATION – sentences begin with a capital letter; capitalize proper nouns
PUNCTUATION – sentences always have end punctuation; quotes around what is said out loud
COMMAS – interjection at beginning of sentence; quote
VOWELS – "ai" digraph; short vowel review
CONSONANTS – initial "b" and "d" sounds; double consonants
VERB TENSE – use of present tense for quote; add "ed" to most verbs to put in past tense; "said" is past tense of irregular verb "to say"
OTHER SKILLS – word practice; name recognition; making a noun plural by adding "s"

S –   oh, Eggbert," s___ ___d _____, "You are a b___ ___ ___. you are not a d___ ___. ba ___ ___ s do not **b___ ___k**.

C –   Oh, Eggbert," sa̲i̲d (*put your name here*), "You are a ba̲ll. You are not a do̲g. Ba̲ll̲s do not **ba̲rk**.

48. car, name, waved, back, window, wave

PARAGRAPH – new person speaking (narrator)
CAPITALIZATION – sentences begin with a capital letter; capitalize proper nouns
PUNCTUATION – sentences always have end punctuation
COMMA – always put commas around "too" if the meaning is "also"
VOWELS – "ow" sound; "au" digraph
CONSONANTS – initial "b" and "c" and "g" sounds
VERB TENSE – add "ed" to most verbs to put in past tense; "was" is past tense of irregular verb "to be";
  "saw" is past tense of irregular verb "to see"
OTHER SKILLS – name recognition; strong verb use

S –   eggbert saw a little girl in a big red **car**. her **name** was _____. the girl **waved**
  and laughed to see the ball in the **back wind**___ ___ of a little yell___ ___ and green **car**.
  eggbert wanted to **wave** and l___ ___gh, too.

C –   Eggbert saw a little girl in a big red **car**. Her **name** was (***put student name here***). The
  girl **waved** and laughed to see the ball in the **back wind<u>ow</u>** of a little yell<u>ow</u> and green **car**.
  Eggbert wanted to **wave** and l<u>au</u>gh, too.

---

49. times, waves, tried, sounded, hiss

PARAGRAPH – topic change
CAPITALIZATION – sentences begin with a capital letter; capitalize proper nouns
PUNCTUATION – sentences always have end punctuation
COMMAS – repeated information; compound sentence
VOWELS – "y"
CONSONANTS – double consonant sounds; plosive "t"
VERB TENSE – add "ed" to most verbs to put in past tense; switch to present tense for narrator aside;
  "tried" is past tense of verb "to try"; "came" is past tense of verb "to come"
OTHER SKILLS – word practice; strong verbs
LITERARY DEVICE – narrator aside; simile

S –   he ___ounce___ up and down, u___ a___d do___ ___, ten **times**. This is how a ba___ ___
  waves to ___ou. eggbe___ ___ **tried** to lau___ ___, but it **sounded** like a hi___ ___.

C –   He b<u>ounced</u> up and down, u<u>p</u> a<u>nd</u> do<u>wn</u>, ten **times**. This is how a ba<u>ll</u> **waves** to <u>y</u>ou.
  Eggbe<u>rt</u> **tried** to lau<u>gh</u>, but it **sounded** like a hi<u>ss</u>.

50. air, hiss, flat

2 PARAGRAPHS – new person speaking; narrator aside
CAPITALIZATION – sentences begin with a capital letter; capitalize proper nouns
PUNCTUATION – sentences always have end punctuation; quotes around what is said out loud
COMMAS – interjection; quote
VOWELS – short vowel review
CONSONANTS – double consonant sounds; plosive "t"
VERB TENSE – add "ed" to most verbs to put in past tense; "said" is past tense of irregular verb "to say"; "was" is past tense of irregular verb "to be"
OTHER SKILL – word recognition
LITERARY DEVICE – narrator aside

S –   "oh, eggbert," said _____. "you will run out of **air** if you **hiss** and

   h__ __ __.

         eggbert *was* looking a little **flat**

C –   "Oh, Eggbert," said (***put your name here***). "You will run out of **air** if you **hiss** and **h̲i̲ss**.
         Eggbert *was* looking a little **flat**.

---

51. window, building, school

2 PARAGRAPHS – new persons speaking
CAPITALIZATION – sentences begin with a capital letter; capitalize proper nouns
PUNCTUATION – sentences always have end punctuation; quotes around what is said out loud
COMMA – quote
VOWELS – short vowel review
CONSONANTS – double consonant sounds; plosive "t"; "s"
VERB TENSE – use of present tense for quote; add "ed" to most verbs to put in past tense; "said" is past tense of irregular verb "to say"; "was" is past tense of irregular verb "to be"; "saw" is past tense of irregular verb "to see"
OTHER SKILLS – homophones "hear/here"; name recognition; color recognition

S –   "here we are," said _____.
         eggbert looked out the back **window**. he saw a big r__ __ **building**. it w__ __ a
   school

C –   "Here we are," said (***put your name here***).
         Eggbert looked out the back **window**. He saw a big r̲e̲d̲ **building**. It w̲a̲s̲ a **school**.

52. school, live, classroom, shelf

PARAGRAPH – new person speaking
CAPITALIZATION – sentences begin with a capital letter; capitalize proper nouns; always capitalize "I"
PUNCTUATION – sentences always have end punctuation; quotes around what is said out loud
COMMA – quote
VOWELS – short vowel review; "y"
CONSONANTS – double consonant sounds; consonant blends; plosive "t"
VERB TENSE – switch to present tense for quote

S –   "___ ___is is our s___ ___ ool," said _____ to eggbert. "you w___ll **live** here in my **classroom**. i have a **shelf** jus___ for you

C –   "This is our **school**," said (*put your name here*) to Eggbert. "You will **live** here in my **classroom**. I have a **shelf** just for you.

---

53. doors, front, school, excited

PARAGRAPH – new person speaking (narrator)
CAPITALIZATION – sentences begin with a capital letter; capitalize proper nouns
PUNCTUATION – sentences always have end punctuation
CONSONANTS – double consonant sounds; plosive "t" and "p"
VERB TENSE – add "ed" to most verbs to put in past tense; "was" is past tense of irregular verb "to be"
OTHER SKILLS – name recognition; strong verb; color recognition

S –   the lady stopped the li___ ___le ye___ ___ow car with the green **doors**. she sto___ ___ed right in **front** of the red **school**. e___ ___bert was very **excited**

C –   The lady stopped the little yellow car with the green **doors**. She stopped right in **front** of the red **school**. Eggbert was very **excited**.

---

54. excited, hissed, flat, picked, back

PARAGRAPH – new subject
CAPITALIZATION – sentences begin with a capital letter; capitalize proper nouns
PUNCTUATION – sentences always have end punctuation
COMMAS – compound sentence; long introductory phrase
CONSONANTS – double consonant sounds; plosive "t"
VERB TENSE – add "ed" to most verbs to put in past tense; "was" is past tense of irregular verb "to be"
OTHER SKILLS – name recognition; strong verb use

S –   eggbert was so **excited**. he bounced, and he **hissed**. he **hi**___ ___**ed** so much, he was almost **flat** when _____ **picked** him up from the **back** of the car

C –   Eggbert was so **excited**. He bounced, and he **hissed**. He **hissed** so much, he was almost **flat** when (*put your name here*) **picked** him up from the **back** of the car.

55. flat, hissed, fix, blow, air, valve

PARAGRAPH – new person speaking

CAPITALIZATION – sentences begin with a capital letter; capitalize proper nouns; always capitalize "I"

PUNCTUATION – sentences always have end punctuation; quotes around what is said out loud

COMMA – quote

VOWELS – short vowel review; "ow" sound; "ou" digraph; double "o" at end of word

CONSONANTS – double consonant sounds; plosive "t"

VERB TENSE – add "ed" to most verbs to put in past tense; "said" is past tense of irregular verb "to say"; "was" is past tense of irregular verb "to be"; future tense with "will"

OTHER SKILLS – word recognition; strong verb use

S –   "you made y___ ___rself **flat**," said _____. "you **hissed** t___ ___ much. i can **fix** that. i will **blow air** into y___ ___r **valve**   "

C –   "You made y<u>ou</u>rself **flat**," said (*put your name here*). "You **hissed** t<u>oo</u> much. I can **fix** that. I will **blow air** into y<u>ou</u>r **valve**."

---

56. could, flat, poor

PARAGRAPH – new person speaking (narrator)

CAPITALIZATION – sentences begin with a capital letter; capitalize proper nouns

PUNCTUATION – sentences always have end punctuation; need question mark at end of question

VOWELS – short vowel review

CONSONANTS – "f" and "t"; "fl" blend

VERB TENSE – add "ed" to most verbs to put in past tense; "was" is past tense of irregular verb "to be"; use of present tense in narrator aside

OTHER SKILL – word recognition

LITERARY DEVICE – narrator aside

S –   eggbert **could** not hiss. he was too **flat**. **poor** eggbert **could** not bounce. he was too ___ ___**at**. do you go **f**___ ___ ___ when you try to talk

C –   Eggbert **could** not hiss. He was too **flat**. **Poor** Eggbert **could** not bounce. He was too <u>**flat**</u>. Do you go <u>**flat**</u> when you try to talk?

57. school, hall, door, a lot, desks

PARAGRAPH – change of topic
CAPITALIZATION – sentences begin with a capital letter; capitalize proper nouns
PUNCTUATION – sentences always have end punctuation
VOWELS – short vowel review; "ow" sound; long vowel review
VERB TENSE – add "ed" to most verbs to put in past tense; "took" is past tense of irregular verb "to take"; "saw" is past tense of irregular verb "to see"
SPELLING RULE – "a lot" is two words
OTHER SKILLS – strong verb use; color recognition; adding "ed" to make past tense of regular verbs

S –   _____ walked into the r___d **school**. she took ___ ___ ___ ___ ___ ___t
d___ ___n a long **hall**. she open___ ___ a br___ ___n **door**. eggbert s___w **a lot** of little **desks**

C –   (*Put your name here*) walked into the r<u>e</u>d **school**. She took <u>Eggbert</u> d<u>ow</u>n a long **hall**.
She open<u>ed</u> a br<u>ow</u>n **door**. Eggbert s<u>aw</u> **a lot** of little **desks**.

---

58. classroom, boys, girls, every, love

PARAGRAPH – new person speaking
CAPITALIZATION – sentences begin with a capital letter; capitalize proper nouns
PUNCTUATION – sentences always have end punctuation; quotes around what is said out loud
COMMA – quote
VOWELS – short vowel review; "y"
CONSONANTS – beginning and middle single consonant sounds; "pl" and "th" blends; initial "w" sound
VERB TENSE – use of present tense in quote; "said" is past tense of irregular verb "to say"; "was" is past tense of irregular verb "to be"; future tense with "will"
OTHER SKILLS – word recognition

S –   "this is our **classroom**," s___e said. "**boys** a___ ___ **girls** co___e here **eve___ ___** day. they
will p___ay w___ ___ ___ you. they w___ ___ ___ **love** you   "

C –   "This is our **classroom**," s<u>he</u> said. "**Boys** a<u>nd</u> **girls** co<u>m</u>e here **every** day. They will p<u>l</u>ay
w<u>ith</u> you. They w<u>i</u>ll **love** you."

59. desk, papers, covered, mess, teacher's

PARAGRAPH – new person speaking (narrator)
CAPITALIZATION – sentences begin with a capital letter; capitalize proper nouns
PUNCTUATION – sentences always have end punctuation; need for question mark after question
CONSONANTS – final double consonants
VERB TENSE – add "ed" to most verbs to put in past tense; "was" is past tense of irregular verb "to be"; use of present tense for narrator aside
OTHER SKILLS – possessive of singular noun; word recognition
LITERARY DEVICE – narrator aside

S –   then she walked up to a big **desk**. many **papers covered** the de___ ___. the **desk**
        w___ ___ a **mess**. is your **teacher's** de___ ___ a **mess**? is your **de**___ ___ a **mess**

C –   Then she walked up to a big **desk**. Many **papers covered** the de<u>sk</u>. The **desk** w<u>as</u> a **mess**.
        Is your **teacher's** de<u>sk</u> a **mess**? Is your de<u>sk</u> a **mess**?

---

60. messy, desk, children, classroom, things, heard, noises

2 PARAGRAPHS – new topics
CAPITALIZATION – sentences begin with a capital letter; capitalize proper nouns
PUNCTUATION – sentences always have end punctuation; quotes around what is said out loud
COMMAS – introductory adverb; quote
VOWELS – review common digraphs
CONSONANTS – double consonant sounds; plosive "t"
VERB TENSE – add "ed" to most verbs to put in past tense; "said" is past tense of irregular verb "to say"; future tense with "will"
OTHER SKILLS – name recognition; word recognition

S –   _____ put eggbert on her **messy desk**. "s___ ___n," she s___ ___d,
        "many **children** will come into this **classr**___ ___**m**."
             eggbert l___ ___ked ar___ ___nd the **classr**___ ___**m**. he saw many funny **things**. He
        h___ ___rd fu___ ___y **noises**

C –   (**Put your name here**) put Eggbert on her **messy desk**. "S<u>oo</u>n," she s<u>ai</u>d, "many
        children will come into this **classr<u>oo</u>m**."
             Eggbert l<u>oo</u>ked ar<u>ou</u>nd the **classr<u>oo</u>m**. He saw many funny **things**. He **heard** fu<u>nn</u>y
        noises.

61. picture, classroom

PARAGRAPH – new person speaking (narrator aside)
CAPITALIZATION – sentences begin with a capital letter; capitalize proper nouns
PUNCTUATION – sentences always have end punctuation; need for question mark after question
VOWELS – "ow" sound and how it varies
CONSONANTS – final "w"
VERB TENSE – switch to present tense for narrator aside
OTHER SKILLS – word recognition; add "s" to make most nouns plural
LITERARY DEVICE – narrator aside

S –   what did eggbert see? draw a **picture** (with some words) of your **classroom** to sh___ ___
       what eggbert saw. h___ ___ many wind___ ___s did ___ ___ ___ ___ ___ ___t see

C –   What did Eggbert see? Draw a **picture** (with some words) of your **classroom** to sh<u>ow</u>
       what Eggbert saw. H<u>ow</u> many wind<u>ows</u> did <u>Eggbert</u> see**?**

---

62. a lot, desks, desk, tried, flat

3 PARAGRAPHS – new topic; new person speaking; narrator again
CAPITALIZATION – sentences begin with a capital letter; capitalize proper nouns; always capitalize "I"
PUNCTUATION – sentences always have end punctuation; quotes around what is said out loud;
       question mark needed at end of question
COMMAS – quote; compound sentence
VOWELS – "ou" blend
CONSONANTS – consonant blends, particularly "nc" and "gg"; plosive "t"
VERB TENSE – switch to present tense for quote; "said" is past tense of irregular verb "to say"; "was" is
       past tense of irregular verb "to be"
SPELLING RULE – "a lot" is two words
OTHER SKILLS – word recognition; counting; reflexive pronouns (myself, himself, etc.)

S –   eggbert saw **a lot** of **desks**. how many d___ ___ ___s did eggbert see
       "i want to bou___ ___e on every **desk**," e___ ___bert said to hi___ ___elf
       he **tried** to bou___ ___e, but he could not. eggbert was too **flat**

C –   Eggbert saw **a lot** of **desks**. How many d<u>esk</u>s did Eggbert see?
       "I want to bou<u>nc</u>e on every **desk**," Eggbert said to hi<u>m</u>self.
       He **tried** to bou<u>nc</u>e, but he could not. Eggbert was too **flat**.

63. lady, need, air, valve, blew

2 PARAGRAPHS – change of topic; new person speaking (narrator)
CAPITALIZATION – sentences begin with a capital letter; capitalize proper nouns; always capitalize "I"
PUNCTUATION – sentences always have end punctuation; quotes around what is said out loud
COMMAS – quote; always put a comma after an interjection; compound sentence
VOWELS – digraphs; "ew" sound
VERB TENSE – switch to present tense for quote; "saw" is past tense of irregular verb "to see"; "said" is
    past tense of irregular verb "to say"; "blew" is past tense of irregular verb "to blow"
OTHER SKILLS – possessive of singular noun; word recognition

S –   the nice **lady** saw eggbert try to b___ ___nce. "oh," she s___ ___d, "I **need** to put **air** into
    y___ ___ "
    the **lady** put eggbert's **valve** up to her lips. she **blew**, and she bl___ ___

C –   The nice **lady** saw Eggbert try to b<u>ou</u>nce. "Oh," she s<u>ai</u>d, "I **need** to put **air** into y<u>ou</u>."
    The **lady** put Eggbert's **valve** up to her lips. She **blew**, and she bl<u>ew</u>.

---

64. fix, blew, air, valve, rolled, tickled

2 PARAGRAPHS – new person speaking; return to narrator
CAPITALIZATION – sentences begin with a capital letter; capitalize proper nouns
PUNCTUATION – sentences always have end punctuation; quotes around what is said out loud
COMMA – quote
VOWELS – "ew" sound
CONSONANTS – consonant blends (lots in this Caught'ya)
VERB TENSE – use of future tense with "will"; "said" is past tense of irregular verb "to say"; "grew" is
    past tense of irregular verb "to grow"
OTHER SKILLS – word recognition; use of strong verbs
LITERARY DEVICE – rhyme

S –   "this will **fix** you," she said to eggbert as she **blew air** into his **valve**.
    eggbert **rolled** in her hands. it **tickled** when _____ **blew air** into his
    valve. he grew and gr___ ___ as she bl___ ___

C –   "This will **fix** you," she said to Eggbert as she **blew air** into his **valve**.
    Eggbert **rolled** in her hands. It **tickled** when (*put your name here*) **blew air** into his
    valve. He grew and gr<u>ew</u> as she **bl<u>ew</u>**.

65. papers, paper, sorry, tickle, times

3 PARAGRAPHS – new topic; new person speaking; back to narrator
CAPITALIZATION – sentences begin with a capital letter; capitalize proper nouns
PUNCTUATION – sentences always have end punctuation; quotes around what is said out loud;
  question mark needed at end of question
COMMAS – quotes
VOWELS – review short vowels; review long vowels
CONSONANTS – "ck" blend
VERB TENSE – add "ed" to form past tense of regular verbs; "said" is past tense of irregular verb "to
  say"; "was" is past tense of irregular verb "to be"
OTHER SKILLS – word recognition; contractions

S –   the nice lady p___cked up some **papers** fr___m h___r desk. one **p___p___r** was right
   under ___ggbert.
       "i'm **sorry**," she said to eggb___rt. "d___d that **tickle** you   "
       eggbert bounced up and ___ ___ ___ ___ three **times** to say, "Y___s   "

C –   The nice lady picked up some **papers** from her desk. One **paper** was right under Eggbert.
       "I'm **sorry**," she said to Eggbert. "Did that **tickle** you?"
       Eggbert bounced up and down three **times** to say, "Yes."

---

66. talk, snake

PARAGRAPH – new subject
CAPITALIZATION – sentences and quotes begin with a capital letter
PUNCTUATION – sentences always have end punctuation; quotes around what is said out loud
COMMAS – quote; commas needed around "too" if meaning is "also"
VOWELS – "ou" blend
CONSONANTS – double consonant blends (there are lots in this Caught'ya)
VERB TENSE – add "ed" to form past tense of regular verbs
OTHER SKILL – word recognition
LITERARY DEVICE – alliteration; simile

S –   the nice lady laughed. e___ ___bert lau___ ___ed, too, with a li___ ___le hiss. he
   wa___ ___ed to say, "Tha___ ___ you," but he cou___ ___ not **talk**. he could only hi___ ___
   like a **snake**

C –   The nice lady laughed. Eggbert laughed, too, with a little hiss. He wanted to say, "Thank
   you," but he could not **talk**. He could only hiss like a **snake**.

67. left, classroom, waved, desk

2 Paragraphs – new topic; new person speaking

Capitalization – sentences and quotes begin with a capital letter; capitalize proper nouns

Punctuation – sentences always have end punctuation; quotes around what is said out loud; question mark needed at end of question

Commas – complex sentence with subordinate clause at beginning (see *Grammar, Usage, and Mechanics Guide*); quote

Vowels – review common digraphs

Consonants – double consonant sounds

Verb tense – "left" is past tense of irregular verb "to leave"; "said" is past tense of irregular verb "to say"; "went" is past tense of irregular verb "to go"

Other skills – word recognition; contractions

S –   then the k___ ___ ___ lady **left** the **classroom**. as she went out the d___ ___r, she **waved** to eggbert.

"g___ ___d-bye," she s___ ___d. "don't fall off ___ ___ ___ **desk**   "

C –   Then the k<u>i</u>nd lady **left** the **classroom**. As she went out the d<u>oo</u>r, she **waved** to Eggbert. "G<u>oo</u>d-bye," she s<u>ai</u>d. "Don't fall off <u>the</u> **desk**."

---

68. tomorrow, door, closed, quiet, classroom

No paragraph – same person speaking; Paragraph – new topic

Capitalization – sentences begin with a capital letter; capitalize proper nouns; always capitalize "I"

Punctuation – sentences always have end punctuation; quotes around what is said out loud

Commas – quote; complex sentence with subordinate clause at beginning

Vowels – review common digraphs

Consonants – "wh" blend

Verb tense – use of future tense with "will"; "said" is past tense of irregular verb "to say"; "was" is past tense of irregular verb "to be"

Other skills – word recognition; reflexive pronouns (myself, himself, etc.)

S – then she s___ ___d, "i will be back **tomorrow** when the sun comes up. be a good ba___ ___   "
___ ___en the **door closed**, it was **quiet** in the **classroom**. ___ ___ ___ ___ ___ ___t was all by hims___ ___ ___

C – Then she s<u>ai</u>d, "I will be back **tomorrow** when the sun comes up. Be a good ba<u>ll</u>."
<u>Wh</u>en the **door closed**, it was **quiet** in the **classroom**. <u>Eggbe</u>rt was all by hims<u>elf</u>.

69. lonely, door, inside, classroom, behind

No PARAGRAPH – same topic

CAPITALIZATION – sentences and quotes begin with a capital letter; capitalize proper nouns;

PUNCTUATION – sentences always have end punctuation; question mark needed at end of question

VOWELS – review of short and long vowels

CONSONANTS – "wh" blend

VERB TENSE – switch to present tense for quote; "saw" is past tense of irregular verb "to see"; "was" is past tense of irregular verb "to be"

OTHER SKILLS – word recognition; question words (where, what, who)

LITERARY DEVICE – narrator aside

S – he was **lonely**. then eggbert saw a **door ins___de** the **classroom**. ___ ___ere d___d it go? w___ ___t was **behind** the **d___ ___r**? w___o was **beh___ ___ ___** the **door**

C – He was **lonely**. Then Eggbert saw a **door ins**<u>i</u>**de** the **classroom**. <u>Wh</u>ere d<u>i</u>d it go? W<u>ha</u>t was **behind** the **d**<u>oo</u>**r**? <u>Wh</u>o was **beh**<u>in</u>**d** the **door?**

---

70. desk, thought, tomorrow

PARAGRAPH – new person speaking

CAPITALIZATION – sentences and quotes begin with a capital letter; capitalize proper nouns; always capitalize "I"

PUNCTUATION – sentences always have end punctuation; quotes around what is said out loud

COMMA – quote

VOWELS – review long and short vowels; "ou" blend and "ai" digraphs

CONSONANTS – consonant blends; "th" blend

VERB TENSE – add "ed" to end of regular verbs to put in past tense; "was" is past tense of irregular verb "to be"; use of future tense with "will"; use of present tense for quote

OTHER SKILL – word recognition

S – "today was a big day for a ball who has never been out___ ___ ___ ___. i will sleep here on the b___g **desk**," **thought** eggbert. "then i w___ll look ar___ ___nd **tomorrow**. i can b___ ___nce and h___ss again now that i am round and full of air ag___ ___n "

C – "Today was a big day for a ball who has never been out<u>side</u>. I will sleep here on the b<u>i</u>g **desk**," **thought** Eggbert. "Then I w<u>i</u>ll look ar<u>ou</u>nd **tomorrow**. I can b<u>ou</u>nce and h<u>i</u>ss again now that I am round and full of air ag<u>ai</u>n."

71. teacher's, desk, next, morning, loud, bell, woke, fell

> **NOTE:** *It is wise to teach first-graders the coordinating conjunctions (for, and, nor, but, or, yet, so). You could have students memorize these conjunctions in a song or by chanting. Then you can tell them never to begin a sentence with one. In a few years, good writers can put them back, but until students learn the judicious use of a fragment, for effect, it is not wise to do so. How many times have you seen a paper where every sentence begins with "and"? You may omit the "and" at the beginning of the following sentences in the student Caught'ya if you feel your students are not yet ready for this skill or leave it in and tell students that four words need to be taken out. Challenge them to find those words.*

2 PARAGRAPHS – new topic; time change

CAPITALIZATION – sentences begin with a capital letter; capitalize proper nouns

PUNCTUATION – sentences always have end punctuation

COMMA – long introductory phrase

VOWELS – review long and short vowels; "ou" blend

CONSONANTS – consonant blends; "nt," "th," and "sk" blends

VERB TENSE – "went," "woke," and "was" are past tense of irregular verbs "to go," "to wake," and "to be"

OTHER SKILLS – never begin a sentence with a conjunction (and); some strong verbs

S –   and eggbert w___ ___t to sleep right there on the **teacher's desk**.
and the **next morning** a **loud bell woke** up ___ ___ ___ ___ ___ ___t. and it was v___ ___y
loud. and eggbert was so surpris___d, he **fell** off the **d**___ ___ ___

C –   Eggbert we<u>nt</u> to sleep right there on the **teacher's desk**.
The **next morning** a **loud bell woke** up <u>Eggbert</u>. It was v<u>e</u>ry **loud**. Eggbert was so
surpri<u>se</u>d, he **fell** off the **d<u>es</u>k**.

---

72. bell, rang, rolled, teacher's, desk, still, classroom

PARAGRAPH – new time

CAPITALIZATION – sentences begin with a capital letter; capitalize proper nouns

PUNCTUATION – sentences always have end punctuation

COMMA – complex sentence with subordinate clause at beginning (see *Grammar, Usage, and Mechanics Guide*)

VOWELS – short "u"

CONSONANTS – consonant blends; "th" blend

VERB TENSE – add "ed" to end of regular verbs to put in past tense; "was" is past tense of irregular verb "to be"

OTHER SKILLS – singular possessive; use of strong verbs

S –   when the **bell rang** again, eggbert **rolled** ___nder the t___ ___ ___ ___er's **desk**. he was
still there when _____ came into the **classroom**

C –   When the **bell rang** again, Eggbert **rolled** <u>u</u>nder the **teacher's desk**. He was **still** there
when (*put your name here*) came into the **classroom**.

73. ready, students

PARAGRAPH – new person speaking
CAPITALIZATION – sentences and quotes begin with a capital letter; capitalize proper nouns
PUNCTUATION – sentences always have end punctuation; quotes around what is said out loud;
   question mark needed at end of question
COMMA – direct address
VOWELS – review short vowels; "ou" blend and "ea" digraphs
CONSONANTS – "wh" blend; "w"
VERB TENSE – add "ed" to end of regular verbs to put in past tense; use of present tense for quote
OTHER SKILLS – word recognition; plurals are formed by adding "s"

S –   "where are you, eggbert?" she called when she d___d n___t see the b___ll. "i want to wash
        you. i m___st g___t you **ready** f___r my **students**   "

C –   "Where are you, Eggbert?" She called when she did not see the ball. "I want to wash you.
        I must get you **ready** for my **students**."

74. everywhere, desks, shelves, bathroom

PARAGRAPH – new topic, new speaker (narrator)
CAPITALIZATION – sentences begin with a capital letter; capitalize proper nouns
PUNCTUATION – sentences always have end punctuation
COMMA – always before "too" when it means "also"
CONSONANTS – "l"
VERB TENSE – add "ed" to end of regular verbs to put in past tense
SPELLING RULE – "too" meaning "also" has two "Os"
OTHER SKILLS – word recognition; compound words

S –   _____ looked **everywhere** for ___ ___ ___bert. she looked under all the
        little **desks**. she looked on all the **shelves**. she looked in the **bath___ ___ ___ ___**, too

C –   (*Put your name here*) looked **everywhere** for Eggbert. She looked under all the little
        desks. She looked on all the **shelves**. She looked in the **bathroom**, too.

> **NOTE:** *After this point, there are fifty more blanks in which you can insert the names of
> your students. There no longer will be a reminder to do so. You will want to use each
> student's name several times.*

75. classroom, teacher

No paragraph – continuation; 2 Paragraphs – narrator; new person speaking
2 Paragraphs – new persons peaking
Capitalization – sentences and quotes begin with a capital letter; capitalize proper nouns
Punctuation – sentences always have end punctuation; quotes around what is said out loud;
    question mark needed at end of question
Commas – noun series; quote
Vowels – review long vowels
Consonants – "wh" blend
Verb tense – add "ed" to end of regular verbs to put in past tense; "said" is past tense of irregular
    verb "to say"; use of present tense for quote
Other skill – name recognition

S – she did not s___ ___ eggbert. "where is that ball?" she said

    just then _____, _____, and _____ c___m___ into the

classroom

    "what are you looking for?" _____ asked her **teacher**

C – She did not s<u>ee</u> Eggbert. "Where is that ball?" she said.

    Just then _____, _____, and _____ c<u>a</u>m<u>e</u> into the

classroom.

    "What are you looking for?" _____ asked her **teacher.**

---

76. teacher, surprise

3 Paragraphs – new persons speaking
Capitalization – sentences and quotes begin with a capital letter; capitalize proper nouns; always
    capitalize "I"
Punctuation – sentences always have end punctuation; quotes around what is said out loud;
    question mark needed at end of question
Commas – quotes
Consonants – consonant blends and doubled consonants
Verb tense – add "ed" to end of regular verbs to put in past tense; "said" is past tense of irregular
    verb "to say"; use of present tense for quote
Other skills – new paragraph needed every time someone new speaks; name recognition

S –   "i am looki___ ___ for eggbert," said the **tea___ ___er**
      "who is e___ ___bert?" a___ ___ed _____.
      "eggbert is a **surprise**," said _____

C –   "I am look<u>ing</u> for Eggbert," said the **teacher.**
      "Who is Eggbert?" a<u>sk</u>ed _____.
      "Eggbert is a **surprise**," said _____.

77. teacher

4 PARAGRAPHS – new persons speaking
CAPITALIZATION – sentences and quotes begin with a capital letter; capitalize proper nouns; always
    capitalize "I"
PUNCTUATION – sentences always have end punctuation; quotes around what is said out loud;
    question mark needed at end of question
COMMAS – quote; always put commas around "too" if the meaning is "also"
VERB TENSE – add "ed" to end of regular verbs to put in past tense; "said" is past tense of irregular
    verb "to say"; use of present tense for quote
OTHER SKILLS – new paragraph needed every time someone new speaks; name recognition

S –   "do you want me to help you look?" asked _____
       "yes," said the **teacher**
       "can i help, too?" asked _____ and _____ as they walked in the door
       "yes, you can help, too," said the **teacher**

C –   "Do you want me to help you look?" asked _____.
       "Yes," said the **teacher.**
       "Can I help, too?" asked _____ and _____ as they walked in the door.
       "Yes, you can help, too," said the **teacher.**

---

78. everywhere, funny-looking, thing, teacher

2 PARAGRAPHS – narrator; new person speaking
CAPITALIZATION – sentences and quotes begin with a capital letter; capitalize proper nouns
PUNCTUATION – sentences always have end punctuation; quotes around what is said out loud;
    question mark needed at end of question
VOWELS – "oo" digraph and "ou" blend; review short vowels
CONSONANTS – consonant blends and doubled consonants
VERB TENSE – add "ed" to end of regular verbs to put in past tense; "came" is past tense of irregular
    verb "to come"; use of present tense for quote
OTHER SKILLS – new paragraph needed every time someone new speaks; name recognition

S –   the six l___ ___ked **everywhere**. just then _____ and _____ came in
       the classr___ ___m d___ ___r.
          "what is that **funny-looking** r___ ___nd **thing** under your desk?" _____ asked
       his **teacher**

C –   The six looked **everywhere**. Just then _____ and _____ came in the
       classroom door.
          "What is that **funny-looking** round **thing** under your desk?" _____ asked his
       teacher.

79. teacher

3 PARAGRAPHS – new persons speaking (second is narrator)
CAPITALIZATION – sentences and quotes begin with a capital letter; capitalize proper nouns
PUNCTUATION – sentences always have end punctuation; quotes around what is said out loud
COMMAS – quote; direct address
VOWELS – "er" sound
VERB TENSE – add "ed" to end of regular verbs to put in past tense; "said" is past tense of irregular verb "to say"
OTHER SKILLS – new paragraph needed every time someone new speaks; name recognition

S –   "that must be eggb___ ___t," said the **teach**___ ___. "come out, eggbert   "
       eggb___ ___t rolled out from und___ ___ her desk.
       "oh, what a pretty ball!" said _____ and _____ togeth___ ___

C –   "That must be Eggb<u>er</u>t," said the **teach<u>er</u>**. "Come out, Eggbert."
       Eggbert rolled out from und<u>er</u> her desk.
       "Oh, what a pretty ball!" said _____ and _____ togeth<u>er</u>.

---

80. bell, rang, children, a lot, noise

PARAGRAPH – new person speaking (narrator)
CAPITALIZATION – sentences begin with a capital letter; capitalize proper nouns
PUNCTUATION – sentences always have end punctuation
COMMA – compound sentence
VERB TENSE – add "ed" to end of regular verbs to put in past tense; "rang" is past tense of irregular verb "to ring"; "ran" is past tense of irregular verb "to run"
SPELLING RULE – "a lot" is 2 words
OTHER SKILLS – possessive of singular noun; name recognition; use of strong verbs

S –   the **bell rang** again, and many **children** ran into the classroom. the **bell** made **a lot** of
       noise. _____ and _____ made **a lot** of **noise**. ___ ___ ___ ___ ___ ___t
       rolled under the t___ ___ ___ ___ er's desk again

C –   The **bell rang** again, and many **children** ran into the classroom. The **bell** made **a lot** of
       noise. _____ and _____ made **a lot** of **noise**. <u>Eggb</u>ert rolled under the
       <u>teach</u>er's desk again.

81. scared, bell, start, school, friends

PARAGRAPH – new person speaking
CAPITALIZATION – sentences and quotes begin with a capital letter; capitalize proper nouns
PUNCTUATION – sentences always have end punctuation; quotes around what is said out loud
COMMAS – direct address; quote
VOWELS – "ou" digraph and blend; "oo" digraph; "ea" digraph
VERB TENSE – "said" is past tense of irregular verb "to say"; imperative tense used to order someone around
SPELLING RULE – "i" before "e" except after "c," and "neighbor," "weigh," and "their" are "weird"
OTHER SKILLS – new paragraph needed every time someone new speaks

S –   "come ___ ___t, eggbert," said the t___ ___cher. "do not be **scared**. it is only the **bell** to **start school**," she s___ ___d. "here are many new **friends**. they want to play with y___ ___   "

C –   "Come <u>ou</u>t, Eggbert," said the t<u>ea</u>cher." Do not be **scared**. It is only the **bell** to **start school**," she s<u>ai</u>d. "Here are many new **friends**. They want to play with y<u>ou</u>."

82. children, sat, quiet, meet, friend

PARAGRAPH – new person speaking (narrator)
CAPITALIZATION – sentences begin with a capital letter; capitalize proper nouns
PUNCTUATION – sentences always have end punctuation
COMMA – repeated word
VOWELS – "ie" and "ei" digraphs
CONSONANTS – "s"
VERB TENSE – add "ed" to end of regular verbs to put in past tense; "sat" is past tense of irregular verb "to sit"; "were" is past tense of irregular verb "to be"
SPELLING RULE – "i" before "e" except after "c," and "neighbor," "weigh," and "their" are "weird"
OTHER SKILL – new paragraph needed every time someone new speaks

S –   all the **children sat** at their desk___. they were very, very **qu**___ ___**t**. they wanted to **meet** eggbert. they wanted to **meet** th___ ___r new **fr**___ ___**nd**

C –   All the **children sat** at their desk<u>s</u>. They were very, very **qu<u>ie</u>t**. They wanted to **meet** Eggbert. They wanted to **meet** th<u>ei</u>r new **fr<u>ie</u>nd**.

83. children, high

PARAGRAPH – change of place
CAPITALIZATION – sentences begin with a capital letter; capitalize proper nouns
PUNCTUATION – sentences always have end punctuation
COMMAS – repeated information; pause
VOWELS – "ou" blend; "ow" sound spelled "ou"; long "i" when followed by "ght"
CONSONANTS – "nc" blend
VERB TENSE – add "ed" to end of regular verbs to put in past tense; "went" is past tense of irregular
    verb "to go"
OTHER SKILLS – possessive of singular noun; use of strong verbs

S –   eggbert rolled out from under the big desk of the teacher. he bounced up and down, up
    and d___ ___ ___ so he could see all the **children**. he b___ ___ ___ ___ ___ ___ so **high**, he
    went right onto the teacher_ ___ desk

C –   Eggbert rolled out from under the big desk of the teacher. He bounced up and down,
    up and d<u>own</u> so he could see all the **children**. He b<u>ounce</u>d so **high**, he went right onto the
    teacher<u>'s</u> desk.

---

84. high, children

NO PARAGRAPH – same place and topic; Paragraph – new person speaks
CAPITALIZATION – sentences and quotes begin with a capital letter; capitalize proper nouns
PUNCTUATION – sentences always have end punctuation; quotes around what is said out loud
COMMAS – extra information; always put commas around "too" if it means "also"; quote
VOWELS – "ou" digraph and "ou" blend; review short vowels
CONSONANTS – consonant blends ("sk" and "rt"); doubled consonants
VERB TENSE – use of present tense for quote
OTHER SKILLS – contraction "it's" means "it is"; new paragraph needed every time someone new
    speaks; name recognition

S – there, up **high** on the big desk, eggbert could see all the **children**. all the **children** c___ ___ld
    see egg___ ___ ___ t, too
        "it's a ball," said _____

C – There, up **high** on the big desk, Eggbert could see all the **children**. All the **children** c<u>ou</u>ld see
    Egg<u>ber</u>t, too.
        "It's a ball," said _____ .

85. special

PARAGRAPH – new person speaking
CAPITALIZATION – sentences and quotes begin with a capital letter; capitalize proper nouns
PUNCTUATION – sentences always have end punctuation; quotes around what is said out loud
COMMAS – quote; appositive (extra information about a noun)
VERB TENSE – "said" is past tense of irregular verb "to say"; use of present tense for quote
OTHER SKILLS – contraction "it's" = "it is"; new paragraph needed every time someone newspeaks; name recognition; reflexive pronouns (himself)

S –   "it's a very **special** ball," said _____, the teacher. this is eggbert.
      __ __ __ __ __ __t can bounce all by h__ __ __ __ __ __ "

C –   "It's a very **special** ball," said _____, the teacher. This is Eggbert. <u>Eggbert</u> can bounce all by <u>himself</u>."

86. through, valve, noises, snake

3 PARAGRAPHS – new persons speaking (first one is narrator)
CAPITALIZATION – sentences and quotes begin with a capital letter; capitalize proper nouns
PUNCTUATION – sentences always have end punctuation; quotes around what is said out loud
COMMAS – always put a comma after an interjection; always put commas around "too" if the meaning is "also"; quote
VOWELS – "oi" blend; review long vowel with silent "e"
CONSONANTS – doubled consonants
VERB TENSE – add "ed" to end of regular verbs to put in past tense; "said" is past tense of irregular verb "to say"; use of present tense for quote
OTHER SKILLS – new paragraph needed every time someone new speaks; name recognition

S –   eggbert hissed **through** his **valve** to say "hello   "
      "oh, he can make **noises**, too," said _____
      "there is a **snake** inside the ball," said _____

C –   Eggbert hissed **through** his **valve** to say "Hello."
      "Oh, he can make **noises**, too," said _____.
      "There is a **snake** inside the ball," said _____.

87. snake, friend

PARAGRAPH – new person speaking

CAPITALIZATION – sentences and quotes begin with a capital letter; capitalize proper nouns

PUNCTUATION – sentences always have end punctuation; quotes around what is said out loud; quote within a quote

COMMAS – introductory word; quote

VOWELS – long vowels with silent "e"

CONSONANTS – "s" sound

VERB TENSE – use of present tense for quote; "said" is past tense of "to say"

SPELLING RULE – "i" before "e"

OTHER SKILLS – new paragraph needed every time someone new speaks; possessive of singular noun; quote within a quote

S –   "no, there is no **___nake** ins___ ___ ___ the ball, " ___aid the teacher. "that i___
         eggbert_ ___ way to ___ay 'Hello.' he want___ to be your **friend**   "

C –   "No, there is no **snake** ins<u>ide</u> the ball," <u>s</u>aid the teacher. "That <u>is</u> Eggbert<u>'s</u> way to <u>s</u>ay
         'Hello.' He want<u>s</u> to be your **friend**."

---

88. patted

PARAGRAPH – new topic (narrator speaking)

CAPITALIZATION – sentences begin with a capital letter; capitalize proper nouns

PUNCTUATION – sentences always have end punctuation

VOWELS – "ou" blend making "ow" sound; review short vowels

CONSONANTS – consonant blends and doubled consonants

VERB TENSE – add "ed" to end of regular verbs to put in past tense

SPELLING RULES – when adding suffix to consonant/vowel/consonant, double the last consonant; compound words

OTHER SKILLS – possessive of singular noun; name recognition; strong verb use

S –   eggbert boun___ ___ ___ off the teacher_ ___ desk. he rol___ ___ ___ and
         boun___ ___ ___ all around the classroom. he b___ ___ ___ ___ ___ ___ by _____
         and by _____. they **patted** him

C –   Eggbert boun<u>ced</u> off the teacher<u>'s</u> desk. He rol<u>led</u> and boun<u>ced</u> all around the classroom.
         He b<u>ounced</u> by _____ and by _____. They **patted** him.

89. kiss, tickled, sneezed, through, valve, sounded, sneeze, kitten

No paragraph – same topic (Eggbert moving around room)
Capitalization – sentences and quotes begin with a capital letter; capitalize proper nouns; always capitalize "I"
Punctuation – sentences always have end punctuation; quotes around what is said out loud
Verb tense – add "ed" to end of regular verbs to put in past tense; "gave" is past tense of "to give"
Other skills – adding "ed" to make a verb past tense; use of strong verbs
Literary device – simile; strong verb use

S – _____ gave eggbert a **kiss**. it **tickl**___ ___. he **sneez**___ ___ **through** his **valve**. it **sound**___ ___ like the **sneeze** of a little **kitten**

C – _____ gave Eggbert a **kiss**. It **tickl**ed. He **sneez**ed **through** his **valve**. It **sound**ed like the **sneeze** of a little **kitten.**

---

90. boys, a lot, threw

Paragraph – change of topic
Capitalization – sentences begin with a capital letter; capitalize proper nouns
Punctuation – sentences always have end punctuation
Vowels – review long vowels with silent "e"
Consonants – consonant blends and doubled consonants
Verb tense – add "ed" to end of regular verbs to put in past tense; "threw" is past tense of irregular verb "to throw"; "was" is past tense of irregular verb "to be"
Spelling rule – "a lot" is 2 words
Other skills – "ed" suffix puts regular verbs in past tense; name and word recognition

S – everyone lau___ ___ ___ ___. _____ and _____, two **boys** who l___k___d to play **a lot**, pick___ ___ up eggbert and **threw** him around the classroom. eggbert l___k___d that. it was f___ ___

C – Everyone laugh_ed. _____ and _____, two **boys** who lik_ed to play **a lot**, pick_ed up Eggbert and **threw** him around the classroom. Eggbert lik_ed that. It was fun.

91. hit, wall, hard

PARAGRAPH – new action
CAPITALIZATION – sentences begin with a capital letter; capitalize proper nouns
PUNCTUATION – sentences always have end punctuation
COMMA – compound sentence
VOWELS – review short vowels
CONSONANTS – "h" sound; consonant blends ("rt" and "st")
VERB TENSE – add "ed" to end of regular verbs to put in past tense; "threw" is past tense of irregular
  verb "to throw"
OTHER SKILLS – new paragraph needed every time someone new speaks; strong verbs; word
  recognition

S –   the boys threw eggbert faster and f___ ___ ___ ___ ___. eggbe___ ___ liked to fly around
   the room, but he did not like it when he **hit** the **wall hard**. it hu___ ___

C –   The boys threw Eggbert faster and <u>faster</u>. Eggbe<u>rt</u> liked to fly around the room, but he did
   not like it when he **hit** the **wall hard**. It hu<u>rt</u>.

---

92. ouch, hit, wall, hard, sorry

2 PARAGRAPHS – new persons speaking
CAPITALIZATION – sentences and quotes begin with a capital letter; capitalize proper nouns
PUNCTUATION – sentences always have end punctuation; quotes around what is said out loud
COMMAS – quotes
CONSONANTS – "h"
VERB TENSE – add "ed" to end of regular verbs to put in past tense; "said" is past tense of irregular
  verb "to say"; use of future tense
OTHER SKILLS – new paragraph needed every time someone new speaks; name recognition

S –   "**ouch**," he ___issed w___en ___e ___it t___e **wall** ___**ard**
   "**sorry**," _____ and _____ said. "we will not do t___at again   "

C –   "**Ouch**," he <u>h</u>issed w<u>h</u>en <u>he</u> **hit** the **wall** <u>h</u>ard.
   "**Sorry**," _____ and _____ said. "We will not do t<u>h</u>at again."

93. mad, boys, hit, wall, hard, threw, slowly

PARAGRAPH – new person speaking (narrator)
CAPITALIZATION – sentences begin with a capital letter; capitalize proper nouns
PUNCTUATION – sentences always have end punctuation
COMMA – introductory phrase
VOWELS – review short vowels; review long vowels with silent "e"; "ai" digraph
VERB TENSE – "threw" is past tense of irregular verb "to throw"; "was" is past tense of irregular verb "to be"
OTHER SKILLS – do not begin a sentence with a coordinating conjunction (for, and, nor, but, or, yet, so); name recognition; review coordinating conjunctions

S –   eggbert was not **mad** at the **boys**. but, he did not l___ ___ ___ to **hit** the **wall hard** because it h___ ___ ___. after that, the **boys threw** eggbert more **slowly**. he did not **hit** the **wall** ag___ ___ ___

C –   Eggbert was not **mad** at the **boys**. He did not l<u>ike</u> to **hit** the **wall hard** because it h<u>urt</u>. After that, the **boys threw** Eggbert more **slowly**. He did not **hit** the **wall** ag<u>ain</u>.

---

94. kiss

PARAGRAPH – time change
CAPITALIZATION – sentences begin with a capital letter; capitalize proper nouns
PUNCTUATION – sentences always have end punctuation; question mark needed at end of question
VOWELS – "ou" blend; review short vowels
CONSONANTS – consonant blends and doubled consonants
VERB TENSE – add "ed" to end of regular verbs to put in past tense; use of present tense for narrator aside; "was" is past tense of irregular verb "to be"
OTHER SKILLS – words within words (compound words); name recognition
LITERARY DEVICE – narrator aside in parentheses

S –   the rest of the day was fun. ___ ___ ___bert rolled a___ ___ ___ ___ ___ the class___ ___ ___ ___. he bounced up to give _____ a ball **kiss**. (What is a ball **kiss** like?)

C –   The rest of the day was fun. <u>E</u>ggbert rolled a<u>round</u> the class<u>room</u>. He bounced up to give _____ a ball **kiss**. (What is a ball **kiss** like?)

95. lap, surprised

No paragraph – same subject; 2 Paragraphs – new persons speaking (2nd is narrator)
Capitalization – sentences and quotes begin with a capital letter; capitalize proper nouns
Punctuation – sentences always have end punctuation; quotes around what is said out loud; question mark needed at end of question
Comma – interjection; quote
Vowels – "oi" and "ou" blends
Verb tense – add "ed" to end of regular verbs to put in past tense
Other skills – singular possessive; new paragraph needed every time someone new speaks; name recognition; strong verbs (narrator)

S – then he b___ ___nced into _____'s **lap**.
"oh," she said, **surprised**. are you g___ ___ng to help me with my work "
eggbert rolled ar___ ___nd in her arms

C – Then he b<u>ou</u>nced into _____'s **lap**.
"Oh," she said, **surprised**. Are you g<u>oi</u>ng to help me with my work?"
Eggbert rolled ar<u>ou</u>nd in her arms.

96. working, hard

No paragraph – same topic; Paragraph – new action
Capitalization – sentences and quotes begin with a capital letter; capitalize proper nouns
Punctuation – sentences always have end punctuation; quotes around what is said out loud
Vowels – "ow" sound
Verb tense – add "ed" to end of regular verbs to put in past tense; "was" is past tense of irregular verb "to be"
Other skills – possessive of singular noun; new paragraph needed every time someone new speaks; name recognition

S – eggbert bounced d___ ___ ___ and rolled up to _____ desk. he was **working hard**. he did not see eggbert.
___ ___ ___ ___ ___ ___t hissed a "Hello." he then rolled to the next desk

C – Eggbert bounced d<u>own</u> and rolled up to _____'s desk. He was **working hard**. He did not see Eggbert.
<u>Eggbert</u> hissed a "Hello." He then rolled to the next desk.

97. need, bath, dirty, bathroom

PARAGRAPH – new action and person speaking
CAPITALIZATION – sentences and quotes begin with a capital letter; capitalize proper nouns; always
   capitalize "I"
PUNCTUATION – sentences always have end punctuation; quotes around what is said out loud
CONSONANTS – consonant blends ("ck," "ld," "sh," "th"); doubled consonants
VERB TENSE – add "ed" to end of regular verbs to put in past tense; use of present tense for quote;
   "told" is past tense of irregular verb "to tell"
OTHER SKILLS – new paragraph needed every time someone new speaks; name recognition

S –   _____ pi__ ___ed up eggbert. "you **need** a **bath**," she told him. "you are
   a very **dirty** ball. i will ca___ ___y you into the **ba__ __room** and wa__ __ you   "

C –   _____ picked up Eggbert. "You **need** a **bath**," she told him. "You are a
   very **dirty** ball. I will ca<u>rr</u>y you into the **ba<u>th</u>room** and wa<u>sh</u> you."

98. idea, a lot, took, bathroom

2 PARAGRAPHS – new person speaking (second is narrator)
CAPITALIZATION – sentences and quotes begin with a capital letter; capitalize proper nouns; always
   capitalize "I"
PUNCTUATION – sentences always have end punctuation; quotes around what is said out loud
COMMAS – quote; always before "too" when it means "also"
VOWELS – "oo" digraph
CONSONANTS – "w" sound
VERB TENSE – add "ed" to end of regular verbs to put in past tense; "said" is past tense of irregular
   verb "to say"; "took" is past tense of verb "to take"
SPELLING RULE – "a lot" is two words; compound words
OTHER SKILLS – new paragraph needed every time someone new speaks; name recognition

S –   "__hat a good **idea**," said the teacher. "i ___anted to ___ash eggbert today, too. he rolled
   around **a lot**   "

   _____ and _____ **took** eggbert into the **bathroom**

C –   "<u>W</u>hat a good **idea**," said the teacher. "I <u>w</u>anted to <u>w</u>ash Eggbert today, too. He rolled
   around **a lot**."

   _____ and _____ **took** Eggbert into the **bathroom.**

99. sink, smelly, soap, getting

NO PARAGRAPH – same topic
CAPITALIZATION – sentences begin with a capital letter; capitalize proper nouns
PUNCTUATION – sentences always have end punctuation
COMMA – compound sentence
VOWELS – double "e" = long "e"; "ea" digraph
CONSONANTS – consonant blends and doubled consonants
VERB TENSE – add "ed" to end of regular verbs to put in past tense; "was" is past tense of irregular verb "to be"
OTHER SKILLS – new paragraph needed every time someone new speaks; color recognition; word recognition
LITERARY DEVICES – alliteration; rhyme

S – they washed __ __ __ __ __ __t in the **sink** with some **smelly soap**. it was gr___ ___n **soap**. eggbert did not like the gr___ ___ n **soap**, but he did like **getting** cl___ ___n

C – They washed <u>Eggbert</u> in the **sink** with some **smelly soap**. It was gr<u>ee</u>n **soap**. Eggbert did not like the gr<u>ee</u>n **soap**, but he did like **getting** cl<u>ea</u>n.

---

100. funny-looking, thing, next, sink, square, tank, water

NO PARAGRAPH – same topic
CAPITALIZATION – sentences begin with a capital letter; capitalize proper nouns
PUNCTUATION – sentences always have end punctuation; question mark needed at end of question
VOWELS – review short vowels
CONSONANTS – consonant blends and doubled consonants
VERB TENSE – "saw" is past tense of irregular verb "to see"; "was" is past tense of irregular verb "to be"
OTHER SKILLS – word recognition
LITERARY DEVICE – narrator aside for humor

S – eggbert saw a **funny-looking thing next** to the **sink**. what was it? it ___ ___ ___ round with a **square tank** at the back. there ___ ___ ___ **water** in it. what ___ ___ ___ it

C – Eggbert saw a **funny-looking thing next** to the **sink**. What was it? It <u>was</u> round with a **square tank** at the back. There <u>was</u> **water** in it. What <u>was</u> it?

101. time, watched

No paragraph – same topic
Capitalization – sentences begin with a capital letter; capitalize proper nouns
Punctuation – sentences always have end punctuation
Commas – prepositional phrase; repetition
Vowels – "ay" digraph; review short vowels
Consonants – "sk" and "rk" blends
Verb tense – add "ed" to end of regular verbs to put in past tense; "was" is past tense of irregular
   verb "to be"; "put" is past tense of irregular verb "to put"
Other skills – name recognition; word recognition

S – eggbert did not have **time** to look. soon he was clean. _____ and _____
   put him on the teacher's desk. from the big d___ ___ ___, eggbert **watched** the class work and
   play, ___ ___ ___ ___ and ___ ___ ___ ___

C – Eggbert did not have **time** to look. Soon he was clean. _____ and _____
   put him on the teacher's desk. From the big d<u>esk</u>, Eggbert **watched** the class work and play,
   <u>work</u> and <u>play</u>.

---

102. walls, hit

Paragraph – change of place
Capitalization – sentences begin with a capital letter; capitalize proper nouns
Punctuation – sentences always have end punctuation
Commas – subordinate clause at beginning; noun series; introductory word
Vowels – "ay" digraph
Consonants – "nt" blend
Verb tense – add "ed" to end of regular verbs to put in past tense; "went" is past tense of irregular
   verb "to go"; use of present tense for quote; "were" is past tense of irregular verb "to be"
Other skills – form past tense with suffix "ed"; name recognition; noun/verb agreement ("were no
   wall<u>s</u>")

S –   when the class went outside, eggbert w___ ___ ___ out, too. _____,
   _____, _____, and _____ played with eggbert. they
   pl___ ___ ___ ___ ball with eggbert. outside, there were no **walls** for eggbert to **hit**

C –   When the class went outside, Eggbert w<u>ent</u> out, too. _____, _____,
   _____, and _____ played with Eggbert. They pl<u>ayed</u> ball with Eggbert.
   Outside, there were no **walls** for Eggbert to **hit**.

103. happy, bell, rang, end, surprised

PARAGRAPH – place change
CAPITALIZATION – sentences begin with a capital letter; capitalize proper nouns
PUNCTUATION – sentences always have end punctuation
COMMAS – complex sentences with subordinate clause at beginning
VOWELS – vowel sounds with "n" ("en" and "an"); long "i" when silent "e"
CONSONANTS – "wh" blend; "n"
VERB TENSE – "rang" is past tense of irregular verb "to ring"; "was" is past tense of verb "to be"
SPELLING RULE – the difference between "when" and "went"
OTHER SKILL – word recognition

S – wh___ ___ the class went in___ ___ ___ ___, eggbert w___ ___t in, too. eggbert was **happy**.
wh___ ___ the **bell** r___ ___g at the **end** of the day, eggbert was **surprised**

C – When the class went inside, Eggbert went in, too. Eggbert was **happy**. When the **bell rang** at the **end** of the day, Eggbert was **surprised.**

---

104. children, left, waved, good-bye, wave

NO PARAGRAPH – continuation of topic
CAPITALIZATION – sentences begin with a capital letter; capitalize proper nouns
PUNCTUATION – sentences always have end punctuation; question mark needed at end of question
VOWELS – short vowel review; "oo" and "oe" digraphs
VERB TENSE – "left" is past tense of irregular verb "to leave"; add "ed" to end of regular verbs to put in past tense
OTHER SKILL – strong verbs (all of them)
LITERARY DEVICE – narrator aside in parentheses

S – all the **ch___ldren left** the cl___ssr___ ___m. th___y **waved good-bye** to eggbert. eggbert g___ve the **children** a ball **wave**. (H___w does s a ball **wave** to you)

C – All the **children left** the classroom. They **waved good-bye** to Eggbert. Eggbert gave the **children** a ball **wave**. (How does a ball **wave** to you?)

105. times, waves, wave

No PARAGRAPH – same topic

CAPITALIZATION – sentences and quotes begin with a capital letter; capitalize proper nouns

PUNCTUATION – sentences always have end punctuation

CONSONANTS – consonant review

VERB TENSE – add "ed" to end of regular verbs to put in past tense; use of present tense for narrator aside

OTHER SKILL – word recognition

LITERARY DEVICE – narrator aside in present tense and parentheses

S – eggbert ___ounced up and down, u___ and ___own ___en (10) **times**. this is ___ow a ___all **waves**. (How do you **wave**? can you show egg___ert how you **wave**   )

C – Eggbert bounced up and down, up and down ten (10) **times**. This is how a ball **waves**. (How do you **wave**? Can you show Eggbert how you **wave**?)

---

106. children, home, good-bye, blew, air

PARAGRAPH – new time

CAPITALIZATION – sentences and quotes begin with a capital letter; capitalize proper nouns

PUNCTUATION – sentences always have end punctuation; quotes around what is said out loud

COMMAS – complex sentence with subordinate clause at beginning; quote

CONSONANTS – consonant review; double consonants

VERB TENSE – "went" is past tense of irregular verb "to go"; "said" is past tense of verb "to say"; add "ed" to end of regular verbs to put in past tense; "blew" is past tense of verb "to blow"

OTHER SKILLS – hyphen use in two words acting as one

S –   after the **children** went **home** for the day, e___ ___ ___ert and the teacher said, "**Good-bye**." the tea___ ___er said, "**Good-bye**," and eggbert hi___ ___ed. before she went **home**, the tea___ ___er **blew** more **air** into e___ ___ ___ert

C –   After the **children** went **home** for the day, Eggbert and the teacher said, "**Good-bye**." The teacher said, "**Good-bye**," and Eggbert hissed. Before she went **home**, the teacher **blew** more **air** into Eggbert.

107. special, children, love, tomorrow

PARAGRAPH – new person speaking
CAPITALIZATION – sentences and quotes begin with a capital letter
PUNCTUATION – sentences always have end punctuation; quotes around what is said out loud
COMMAS – quote; compound sentence
VOWELS – long vowel sounds (doubled if end of 2-letter word)
VERB TENSE – use of present tense for quote; use of imperative
OTHER SKILLS – contraction "you're" = "you are"

S –   "you're a **special** ball," she said. "my **children love** you. be a good ball. g___ to sl___ ___p
on my desk, and w___ will be back **tomorrow**   "

C –   "You're a **special** ball," she said. "My **children love** you. Be a good ball. G<u>o</u> to sl<u>ee</u>p on
my desk, and w<u>e</u> will be back **tomorrow**."

---

108. night, lonely

PARAGRAPH – narrator speaking
CAPITALIZATION – sentences begin with a capital letter; capitalize proper nouns
PUNCTUATION – sentences always have end punctuation
COMMA – subordinate clause
VERB TENSE – "was" is past tense of irregular verb "to be"; add "ed" to end of regular verbs to put in
     past tense
OTHER SKILLS – possessive of singular noun; name recognition; strong verb use

S –   that **night**, eggbert was **lonely** again. he could not sleep. he rolled around the classroom.
he bounced onto _____ desk

C –   That **night**, Eggbert was **lonely** again. He could not sleep. He rolled around the
classroom. He bounced onto _____'s desk.

---

109. messy, bathroom, dark

NO PARAGRAPH – same topic
CAPITALIZATION – sentences begin with a capital letter; capitalize proper nouns
PUNCTUATION – sentences always have end punctuation
VOWELS – long "i" followed by "ght"
CONSONANTS – "ght" (go over other words like "night," right," "might")
VERB TENSE – "was" is past tense of irregular verb "to be"; add "ed" to end of regular verbs to put in
     past tense
OTHER SKILL – possessive of singular noun

S – the teacher_ ___ desk was **messy**. eggbert rolled into the **bathroom**. it was **dark** inside. the
li___ ___ ___ was off

C – The teacher<u>'s</u> desk was **messy**. Eggbert rolled into the **bathroom**. It was **dark** inside. The
li<u>ght</u> was off.

110. toilet, wet

No PARAGRAPH – same topic
CAPITALIZATION – sentences begin with a capital letter; capitalize proper nouns
PUNCTUATION – sentences always have end punctuation
COMMA – pause
CONSONANTS – "gh" blend
VERB TENSE – add "ed" to end of regular verbs to put in past tense; "was" is past tense of irregular verb "to be"
OTHER SKILL – word recognition
LITERARY DEVICE – humor

S – eggbert bounced up and ___ ___, higher and __ __ __ __ __ __. he __ __ __ __ __ __ __ right into the **toilet**! it was **wet** and cold

C – Eggbert bounced up and <u>up</u>, higher and <u>higher</u>. He <u>bounced</u> right into the **toilet**! It was **wet** and cold.

---

111. toilet, water, slept, night

No PARAGRAPH – same topic
CAPITALIZATION – sentences begin with a capital letter; capitalize proper nouns
PUNCTUATION – sentences always have end punctuation
VERB TENSE – "slept" is past tense of irregular verb "to sleep"; "was" is past tense of verb "to be"
OTHER SKILLS – word recognition; negatives

S – eggbert could not bounce out of the **toilet**. he could not __ __ __ __ __ __ out of **water**. he **slept** in the **toilet** all **night**. it was wet and c__ __ __

C – Eggbert could not bounce out of the **toilet**. He could not <u>bounce</u> out of **water**. He **slept** in the **toilet** all **night**. It was wet and <u>cold</u>.

---

112. school, early, door

PARAGRAPH – time change
CAPITALIZATION – sentences begin with a capital letter; capitalize proper nouns
PUNCTUATION – sentences always have end punctuation
COMMAS – noun series; compound sentence
VERB TENSE – "came" is past tense of irregular verb "to come"; add "ed" to end of regular verbs to put in past tense
OTHER SKILLS – name recognition; add "ed" suffix to form past tense of regular verbs; strong verb use

S –   the next morning the teacher and _____, _____, and _____ ___ came to **school early**. they open___ ___ the **door** of the classroom. they look___ ___ and look___ ___, but they did not see eggbert

C –   The next morning the teacher and _____, _____, and _____ ___ came to **school early**. They open<u>ed</u> the **door** of the classroom. They look<u>ed</u> and look<u>ed</u>, but they did not see Eggbert.

113. shelves, cubbies

PARAGRAPH – slight change of topic
CAPITALIZATION – sentences begin with a capital letter; capitalize proper nouns
PUNCTUATION – sentences always have end punctuation; question mark needed at end of question
VERB TENSE – "was" is past tense of irregular verb "to be"; add "ed" to end of regular verbs to put in
     past tense
SPELLING RULE – form plural of nouns ending in "y" by changing the "y" to "i" and adding "es"
OTHER SKILLS – name recognition; word recognition

S –   where was he? _____ looked in all the **shelves** and **cubbies**.
            _____ looked under all the desks. the teacher ___ ___ ___ ___ ___ ___ up high

C –   Where was he? _____ looked in all the **shelves** and **cubbies**.
            _____ looked under all the desks. The teacher <u>looked</u> up high.

114. heard, splash, bathroom, children

NO PARAGRAPH – continuation
CAPITALIZATION – sentences begin with a capital letter; capitalize proper nouns
PUNCTUATION – sentences always have end punctuation; question mark needed at end of question
VERB TENSE – "was" is past tense of verb "to be"; "heard" is past tense of irregular verb "to hear"; "ran"
     is past tense of the verb "to run"
SPELLING RULE – compound words
OTHER SKILLS – word recognition; name recognition

S –   it was not funny. where was eggbert? then _____ **heard** a **splash** in the **bathroom**.
     all three **children** ran into the **bath**__ __ __ __

C –   It was not funny. Where was Eggbert? Then _____ **heard** a **splash** in the
     bathroom. All three **children** ran into the **bath<u>room</u>**.

115. toilet, sink, smelly, soap

No paragraph – continuation; 2 Paragraphs – new persons speaking
Capitalization – sentences and quotes begin with a capital letter; capitalize proper nouns
Punctuation – sentences always have end punctuation; quotes around what is said out loud
Commas – quotes
Verb tense – "said" is past tense of irregular verb "to say"; use of present tense for quote; add "ed" to end of regular verbs to put in past tense
Other skills – word recognition; name recognition; new paragraph needed every time someone new speaks; strong verb use

S – there was eggbert in the **toilet**.
　　"this is no place for a ball," said _____. she picked ___ ___ ___ ___ ___ ___t up
　　from the t___ ___ ___ ___t and washed him in the **sink** with the **smelly** green **soap**
　　"ewww," said _____

C – There was Eggbert in the **toilet**.
　　"This is no place for a ball," said _____. She picked <u>Eggbert</u> up from the **toilet**
　　and washed him in the **sink** with the **smelly** green **soap.**
　　"Ewww," said _____.

---

116. rest, happy, kiss, boy, girl

Paragraph – back to narrator
Capitalization – sentences begin with a capital letter; capitalize proper nouns
Punctuation – sentences always have end punctuation
Vowels – review short vowels; "oo" digraph
Consonants – doubled consonants
Verb tense – "came" is past tense of irregular verb "to come"; "was" is past tense of irregular verb "to be"; add "ed" to end of regular verbs to put in past tense
Spelling rules – compound words; plurals of words not ending in "s"
Other skills – word recognition; compound words; adding the suffix "ed" to form past tense

S – 　the **rest** of the ___ ___ildren came into the class___ ___ ___ ___. eggbert was **happy** again.
　　he bounced up to give a ball **kiss** to every **boy** and **girl**. all day he ___ ___ ___ ___ ___ ___ ___
　　and r___ ___ ___ ___ ___ around the ___ ___ ___ ___ ___room

C – 　The **rest** of the <u>children</u> came into the class<u>room</u>. Eggbert was **happy** again. He bounced
　　up to give a ball **kiss** to every **boy** and **girl**. All day he <u>bounced</u> and <u>rolled</u> around the
　　<u>class</u>room.

117. bell, rang, end, good-bye, idea

2 PARAGRAPHS – time change; new person speaking
CAPITALIZATION – sentences and quotes begin with a capital letter; capitalize proper nouns; always capitalize "I"
PUNCTUATION – sentences always have end punctuation; quotes around what is said out loud
COMMAS – complex sentence with subordinate clause at beginning; quote
VOWELS – "ay" digraph; "oo" digraph; "ai" digraph
VERB TENSE – "rang" is past tense of irregular verb "to ring"
OTHER SKILLS – word recognition; new paragraph needed every time someone new speaks;

S –   when the **bell rang** at the **end** of the d___ ___, eggbert did not want to say "**Good-bye.**"
    the children did not want to say "G___ ___ ___-___ ___ ___ "
      "i have an **idea**," s___ ___ ___ the kind teacher

C –   When the **bell rang** at the **end** of the day, Eggbert did not want to say "**Good-bye.**" The children did not want to say "**Good-bye.**"
      "I have an **idea**," said the kind teacher.

---

118. idea, lonely, night

PARAGRAPH – narrator aside
CAPITALIZATION – sentences begin with a capital letter; capitalize proper nouns
PUNCTUATION – sentences always have end punctuation; question mark needed at end of question
CONSONANTS – "wh" blend
VERB TENSE – "was" is past tense of irregular verb "to be"
OTHER SKILLS – possession of singular noun; name recognition
LITERARY DEVICE – narrator aside

S –   ___ ___at was the teacher's **idea**? would eggbert be **lonely** again? ___ ___ere could
       ___ ___ ___ ___ ___ ___t sleep every **night**

C –   What was the teacher's **idea**? Would Eggbert be **lonely** again? Where could Eggbert sleep every **night?**

119. home, tonight, tomorrow, night, next

PARAGRAPH – new person speaking

CAPITALIZATION – sentences and quotes begin with a capital letter; capitalize proper nouns; always capitalize "I"

PUNCTUATION – sentences always have end punctuation; quotes around what is said out loud; question mark needed at end of question

COMMA – quote

VOWELS – long vowels with silent "e"; long "i" with "ght"

VERB TENSE – use of present tense for quote

SPELLING RULE – difference between homophones "know/no"

OTHER SKILLS – word recognition; new paragraph when someone new speaks; name recognition

S –   "i know what to do," said _____. "eggbert can come **home** with me **tonight**. he can go h___ ___ ___ with _____ **tomorrow night**. who will t___ ___ ___ eggbert **home** the **next** n___ ___ ___ ___

C –   "I know what to do," said _____. "Eggbert can come **home** with me **tonight**. He can go **h<u>o</u>me** with _____**tomorrow night**. Who will t<u>ake</u> Eggbert **home** the **next n<u>ig</u>ht?**"

---

120. idea, school, night, home, boy, girl, happy

PARAGRAPH – new topic

CAPITALIZATION – sentences and quotes begin with a capital letter; capitalize proper nouns

PUNCTUATION – sentences always have end punctuation

COMMAS – always put commas around "too" if it means "also"

VOWELS – review short and long vowels

CONSONANTS – review consonants

VERB TENSE – "was" is past tense of irregular verb "to be"; add "ed" to end of regular verbs to put in past tense; "went" is past tense of irregular verb "to go";

OTHER SKILL – word recognition

S –   That was the teacher's **idea**, too. every day eggbert b___ ___ ___ ___ ed, r___ ___ ___ ed, read, w___ ___ ___ed, and pl___ ___ed at **school**. every **night** he went **home** with a **boy** or **girl**. ___ ___ ___ ___ ___ ___t was a very **happy** ___ ___ ___ ___

C –   That was the teacher's **idea**, too. Every day Eggbert b<u>ounce</u>d, r<u>olle</u>d, read, w<u>orke</u>d, and pl<u>ay</u>ed at **school**. Every **night** he went **home** with a **boy** or **girl**. E<u>ggber</u>t was a very **happy** b<u>all</u>.

The End

Now make up your own story about Eggbert and your class.
Where will Eggbert be found next? Where will he bounce?

BIBLIOGRAPHY

♥ RESOURCE CONTAINS GOOD SUGGESTIONS FOR WRITING

Caplan, Rebekah and Catherine Keech. *Showing Writing: A Training Program to Help Students Be Specific.* Berkeley, CA: University of California Press, 1980.

Dierking, Connie Campbell and Sherra Ann Jones. *Growing Up Writing: Mini-Lessons for Emergent and Beginning Writers.* Gainesville, FL: Maupin House Publishing, 2003. ♥

Elgin, Suzette Haden. "The Great Grammar Myth." National Writing Project Occasional Paper #5. Berkeley, CA: University of California Press, 1982.

Forney, Melissa. *Dynamite Writing Ideas! Empowering Students to Become Authors.* Gainesville, FL: Maupin House Publishing, 1996. ♥

___. *Razzle Dazzle Writing: Achieving Success Through 50 Target Skills.* Gainesville, FL: Maupin House Publishing, 2001. ♥

___. *The Writing Menu: Ensuring Success for Every Student.* Gainesville, FL: Maupin House Publishing, 1999. ♥

Freeman, Marcia S. *Building a Writing Community: A Practical Guide.* Gainesville, FL: Maupin House Publishing, 1995. ♥

___. *Listen to This: Developing an Ear for Expository.* Gainesville, FL: Maupin House Publishing, 1997. ♥

___. *Teaching the Youngest Writers: A Practical Guide.* Gainesville, FL: Maupin House Publishing, 1998. ♥

Hacker, Diane. *A Writer's Reference (Third Edition).* Boston: Bedford Books, 1995.

Haley-James, Shirley and John Warren Stewig. *Houghton Mifflin English.* Boston: Houghton Mifflin, 1988.

Johnson, Bea. *Never Too Early to Write: Adventures in the K-1 Writing Workshop.* Gainesville, FL: Maupin House Publishing, 1999. ♥

Kiester, Jane. *Blowing Away the State Writing Assessment Test.* Gainesville, FL: Maupin House Publishing, 1996. ♥

___. *Caught'ya! Grammar with a Giggle.* Gainesville, FL: Maupin House Publishing, 1990.

___. *Caught'ya Again! More Grammar with a Giggle.* Gainesville, FL: Maupin House Publishing, 1992. ♥

___. *The Chortling Bard: Grammar with a Giggle for High Schools.* Gainesville, FL: Maupin House Publishing, 1997.

___. *Elementary, My Dear! Grammar with a Giggle for Grades 1, 2, and 3.* Gainesville, FL: Maupin House Publishing, 2000.

___. *Giggles in the Middle: Caught'ya! Grammar with a Giggle for Middle School.* Gainesville, FL: Maupin House Publishing, 2006.

___. *Juan and Marie Join the Class: Caught'ya! Grammar with a Giggle for Third Grade.* Gainesville, FL: Maupin House Publishing, 2006.

___. *Putrescent Petra Finds Friends: Caught'ya! Grammar with a Giggle for Second Grade.* Gainesville, FL: Maupin House Publishing, 2006.

Laird, Charlton, preparer. *Webster's New World Thesaurus.* New York: Simon and Schuster, 1985.

Sherwin, J. Stephen. *Four Problems in Teaching English: A Critique of Research.* Scranton, PA: International Textbook Company, 1969.

Sitton, Rebecca and Robert Forest. *Quick-Word Handbook for Beginning Writers.* North Billerica, MA: Curriculum Associates, 1994. ♥

Stein, Jess, ed. *The Random House Dictionary of the English Language (Unabridged Edition).* New York: Random House, 1967.

Warriner, John, and Sheila Laws Graham. *Warriner's English Grammar and Composition, Complete Course.* New York: Harcourt Brace Jovanovich, 1957.

___. *Warriner's English Grammar and Composition, Third Course.* New York: Harcourt Brace Jovanovich, 1977.

Wong, Harry K. and Rosemary T. Wong. *The First Days of School: How to Be an Effective Teacher.* Mountain View, CA: Harry K. Wong Publications, 1998.